The Tribulation
What I Was Shown!

By Tony Lamb

I have been shown more about the Tribulation than any other man alive!

Introduction

Welcome to 'The Tribulation'!

Matthew 24:21
For then shall be great tribulation, such as was not since the beginning of the world to this time, no, nor ever shall be

Matthew 24: 42
Watch therefore: for ye know not what hour your Lord doth come.

Matthew 24: 51
There shall be weeping and gnashing of teeth.

Matthew 25: 10
And the door was shut.

Matthew 24:4 to 13
And Jesus answered and said unto them, Take heed that no man deceive you.

[5]For many shall come in my name, saying, I am Christ; and shall deceive many.

And ye shall hear of wars and rumors of wars: see that ye be not troubled: for all these things must come to pass, but the end is not yet.

For nation shall rise against nation, and kingdom against kingdom: and there shall be famines, and pestilences, and earthquakes, in divers places.

All these are the beginning of sorrows.

Then shall they deliver you up to be afflicted, and shall kill you: and ye shall be hated of all nations for my name's sake.

And then shall many be offended, and shall betray one another, and shall hate one another.

And many false prophets shall rise, and shall deceive many.

And because iniquity shall abound, the love of many shall wax cold.

But he that shall endure unto the end, the same shall be saved.

Matthew 24: 36
But of that day and hour knoweth no man, no, not the angels of heaven, but my Father only.

Matthew 24: 42
Watch therefore: for ye know not what hour your Lord doth come.

We are in the Time of Sorrow (Birth Pangs). Look at the world you know it to be true. A woman in labor going through labor pains will tell you the labor pains start mild, but increase in intensity and frequency until the baby is born.

And right now, our pains are increasing, and coming closer and closer together and getting stronger and stronger. And then the baby is born. But this baby will be the Rapture of the faithful.

But it is NOT just the faithful it will also be children, babies even babies in the womb, EXCEPT for those who have received the shot that changes their DNA.

In many of my dreams, I saw children and even babies who were IN the Tribulation, and I thought either my dreams were in error or there was something I was not understanding about the Rapture.

I was perplexed by this and I was afraid my dreams were in error. And I knew that God does not make mistakes. So, I prayed and I prayed on this and finally the Holy Spirit revealed it to me that heaven was for the pure without spot of blemish.

And these small children and babies I was shown in my dreams had their DNA changed and so they were not pure in their seed, they were found with a spot, a wrinkle.

Even though they could NOT make heaven their home God being a merciful God did make provision for the innocent. Those who were young or old or who were forced to have an injection that changed their DNA. And that provision was called (Abraham's Bosom).

This was intended to be a temporary holding place for the early saints, before there was a heaven for them to go to.

Now it would be a place where those who were forced to change their DNA could go, and it would not be heaven, and it would not be hell.

A place in between heaven and hell called Abraham's Bosom.

I had prayed on this several times over several years and this is what the Holy Spirit told me. So, I have this on the highest authority.

Remember heaven is for those found without a spot or a wrinkle, pure and forgiven.

And when you change your DNA you are no longer made in God's image, but you then become made in man's image.

Remember God already destroyed the earth before, and for the very same reason as the people ended up changing their DNA through the fallen angels, only Noah and his family were pure in their SEED (their DNA).

And these fallen angels corrupted all of the (seed) or DNA of mankind and most of the animals, except for Noah and his family and the animals in the Ark.

So, God destroyed the earth including every animal that walked, crawled or flew upon the earth.

And God will destroy the earth again, and for the very same reason.

I have had so much more than just dreams and visions, I have had much contact with the Holy Spirit, he comes to me and tell me things He wants me to know and tell you WHAT IS TO COME, and when I have a question I pray, and many times the Holy Spirit will give me my answer.

But I do NOT always get my answer and NOT all things are to be revealed.

I normally hear the Holy Spirit like a voice in my head, or in dreams and on several occasions, I heard His voice with my own ears. I know, I recognize the Holy Spirits voice as I have heard it many times.

I have had an absolute flood of Tribulation dreams and visions; they started in late 2013. They started with a very big bang and year by year they have slowed down until now I may only get a prophetic dream once every month or two.

But all I was shown about the Tribulation put a fear in me, it terrified me to my very core. I wanted to run and hide BUT there was no hiding from what is to come.

Everything I was shown, I thought it was coming soon in a year or two, but 9 years later we are still here. BUT now, just now I am starting to see the pieces to just now fall into place, it is the beginning of something more horrible, more tragic than words can describe, but I will make every attempt to do so here.

I have made videos about the Tribulation, and what was to come but I did not have the time to describe everything. And I did not know how graphic I could make my videos. I would tend to describe one or two aspects and then the next video I would tell more.

Here I can take the time to get into details that I could not possibly do on any video.

Yes, I have seen the Tribulation and God showed me more of the Tribulation than any other man or woman alive.

My dreams filled me with terror, and I saw much horror and I wept bitterly at the sights I was shown.

Tears fell like rain and formed puddles and I trembled at the sights I beheld and all I could say was:

A LOT OF PEOPLE ARE GOING TO GET HURT!   I KNOW BECAUSE I HAVE SEEN IT!

CHAPTER ONE
My Calling

I probably had the hardest calling I have ever heard of. A few months after my dreams of the Tribulation started the Holy Spirit came to me and ASKED me to be a Watchman.

I really didn't know what a watchman was or what he even did. I was shown Ezekiel 33 verses 3 to 9 with an emphasis on verse 6.

Ezekiel 33:6
But if the watchman see the sword come, and blow not the trumpet, and the people be not warned; if the sword come, and take any person from among them, he is taken away in his iniquity; but his blood will I require at the watchman's hand.

This concerned me greatly and I was afraid. But then the Holy Spirit said I would speak and tell the people about my dreams and what had happened to me and WARN the people as to what was coming.

I tried to tell the Holy Spirit I was NOT a public speaker and I could NOT do what He asked of me.

This went on for several weeks and almost every night the Holy Spirit came to me and asked me to be a Watchman, and to speak and every night I said: Please NOT me Lord, I can not do what you ask of me, Please Lord.

The Holy Spirit just kept on asking me to be a Watchman and to SPEAK. And I kept on saying that I could not speak in front of an audience.

The Holy Spirit told me that I was to be a Watchman for Jesus and warn the people.

I started seeing Watchman videos on youtube (when I didn't even do a search for Watchmen). I had no idea what a Watchman did and I had no interest in being a Watchman.

I prayed; Lord, who am I, that anyone should listen to me, I am not a Minister, Deacon, or even a Sunday School teacher. But the Lord was persistent and told me: "**I choose you'**.

But I said: '**Lord, NO NOT ME, PLEASE NOT ME'**.

This went on for several weeks and almost every night with me sobbing and telling the Lord NO, that I could not do it, as I was NOT a public speaker.
But the Holy Spirit told me: '**Moses was not a public speaker either, as he had a**

very bad stutter, so I was in good company'.

On Feb. 28, 2015, I had knee replacement surgery on my left knee and after 4 months I was still walking with a cane and limping around but I was making progress, but it was slow.

THEN in the morning of June 28, 2015 with tears streaming down my face I relented and I told God, '**I would try**' to give his message that He put in my heart to speak.
That was NOT the answer God was looking for. As TRY is what you say when you DO NOT DO A THING you will always say: I TRIED!

With God YOU DO, or you do not do a thing, THERE IS NO TRY!

Four hours later I woke up at 6 AM as I could not sleep, I got up out of bed and went into the kitchen to make coffee. I stepped onto a wet spot on my kitchen floor and both my feet went out from under me and I fell on my kitchen floor onto the very same knee I had surgery on 4 months to the day before.

I laid on my kitchen floor screaming in pain until the ambulance took me to the hospital, and they gave me a shot of morphine to calm me down.

I know what you are thinking, that it was just a coincidence. But I am reminded that there are NO coincidences when it comes to God. It was exactly 4 hours after I in effect told God (NO again) that I found myself sprawled out on my kitchen floor screaming in pain.

NOW you may think God could never harm or hurt anyone, but I remind you of the flood of Noah and Sodom and Gomorrah only two instances. God is God and God will do all His pleasure. IF God will not accept your NO answer, God will get your attention one way or another.

WELL, that morning God GOT MY ATTENTION. And God made me an offer that I could not refuse.

The doctors at the hospital said it was a miracle that I did NOT break anything or dislodge the implant in my fall, another miracle. But I did tare almost every ligament in my left knee.

Then there is this, about 6 weeks after my fall on my kitchen floor, the Holy Spirit

again comes to me and reminds me that:
'**You do not need to walk to do God's will**'.

That was like an electric shock hitting me and I realized that the next time I tell God NO I just might not survive the punishment.

I was reminded that Moses had a very bad stutter and was NOT a public speaker either SO I WAS IN GOOD COMPANY.

I was told I had a connection to Jonah as Jonah also told God NO and he ran from God. But Jonah ended up in Nineveh, just like I ran from God and we both ended up in our Nineveh.

When God wants you for a work, God will NOT accept your NO answer. If you try to reason or argue with God you lose before you even start your argument.

I was told I had a connection with Noah as Noah was a preacher, and for 120 years, Noah had only ONE message and every Sabbath he preached his same message. Noah preached to repent of sin and enter the Ark for safety. But no one came to hear him preach (except his family) and no one entered the Ark except for Noah and his family

I also only have JUST ONE message:
REPENT FOR THE KINGDOM OF HEAVEN IS AT HAND.

The very first time I stood up in my church, I SPOKE what the Holy Spirit had given me to speak. With tears rolling down my face as I was terrified what would happen IF I DIDN'T speak.

I told of a time coming called the Time of Sorrows or (Birth Pains) and all the calamities that would be coming, war, earthquakes, riots, looting, lawlessness, many fires, food would increase, in price and get so expensive people could not afford to hardly eat, and meat would become scarce and very expensive.

Food would just keep going up and up and up and become even more scarce until one day you could NOT buy food at any price.

Energy, gas, electricity, propane, all forms of energy would go to astronomical rates and just keep rising. There would be power outages here and there and one day there would be NO MORE POWER.

Our economy would totally collapse and our cash would become worthless paper.

Banks would keep closing and eventually ALL banks would close, and then debit and credit cards and checks would be worthless. I warned them that a NEW digital currency would then be introduced, but it still would not help the economy. I warned them to get any extra cash out of the bank and anything of value out of a safety deposit box because when the banks close you will lose it all.

The only money you will have will be what is in your pocket and that will quickly go to zero in value within only a week or two.

Everything paper would be totally worthless, stocks, bonds, insurance policies and the government would default bringing much chaos to America, then everyone would hit the streets and mob rule would come to America. Riots, food riots, energy riots, food stamp riots, everyone would be rioting for some reason and the mobs would take over the country and much fires, looting until the entire country seems to have gone mad and many people will kill for no reason.

Earthquakes, tsunamis would kill many thousands of people.

There would be flooding in parts of the country, and serious drought in other parts of the country.

There will be no police, no fire departments no ambulances, no hospitals, and IF you get in trouble NO ONE WILL CARE AND NO ONE WILL COME TO HELP YOU. And neighbor would turn against neighbor and family members against family.

Who will work anywhere when they are afraid to leave their home unprotected and besides NO ONE is getting paid, so NO ONE WORKS.

That holds true for everyone even power plant operators will not show up for work if they are not getting paid in one form or another that actually has any value.

Gold & silver will become worthless as they can NOT feed you or keep you warm.

People would go mad and do unspeakable things.

Only food, clean water, medications, propane, firewood, medical supplies, camping supplies and the like will have any real value in a barter society. As that is where we are headed. Everything will be by barter & swap.

Then I proceeded to tell them what was coming in the Tribulation, all the horrors, I WAS SHOWN.

I told them about fallen angels walking the earth again and killing 1/3 of mankind.

Revelation 9: 14 & 15.

Saying to the sixth angel which had the trumpet, Loose the four angels which are bound in the great river Euphrates.

[15] And the four angels were loosed, which were prepared for an hour, and a day, and a month, and a year, for to slay the third part of men.

I told them about famine coming and how people would resort to eating bugs, grass, leaves anything to ease their hunger pains.

 I told them about pestilences and diseases that were coming would destroy over one billion people. Remember this was in 2015.

I told them about a massive earthquake so powerful, that would hit the west coast of America that it would cause other earthquakes to rupture and first earthquake would be a 9.4 or greater. It would start in the Cascadia rift area off Calif., Oregon & Washington coast.

Then there would be a massive tsunami so huge and so powerful that it would cause a change in the earth's rotation speed and it would shorten our day.

This earthquake would cause a chain reaction of earthquakes followed by massive earthquakes in Calif. From the Bay area down to San Diego. The entire West coast will be destroyed.

The New Madrid fault in southern Missouri would rupture causing a rift in the Mississippi river basin and basically divide America from top to bottom.

Then an asteroid would strike in the Atlantic Ocean and cause a tsunami hundreds of feet high to hit the entire East coast of America.

And all this earthquake and tsunami activity would cause the earth to reel to and fro like a drunkard and change the length of the day. Isaiah 24:20.

War was coming to America and I saw foreign troops on American soil, I saw nuclear weapons being detonated over several large American cities.

I told them all this with tears streaming down my face because the Holy Spirit told me to SPEAK and I knew America would be destroyed.

So, I spoke. But I think most of them didn't believe me. The pastor spoke up and said America was so big that if one area could NOT produce food there would be other areas that would produce food and enough for all American's.

So 9 years later how is that theory holding up?

You may think this book is full of hate, horror and rage. But NO this book is about love, forgiveness and the love and saving grace of Jesus Christ. And there are things you need to know and address about the coming Tribulation and most important how to avoid the Tribulation.

How you avoid the Tribulation is to be Rapture ready: before the Tribulation.

I told my church I fully believed in the pre-tribulation rapture, but I didn't know the sequence and the timing of these events, and we needed to be prepared in case we had to live on what we had at home or the cash in our pocket.

I told them that we just may see some calamities before we get Raptured out of here and the most important thing, we could do was to prepare with Jesus first and food & water second.

Also, if we were Raptured before any serious events came then we all had family, friends, neighbors who were NOT Rapture ready and they would desperately need our stored supplies.

I think this message fell on deaf ears, no one said anything about my message, NOT A WORD and you could have heard a pin drop when I finished.

BUT I did as the Holy Spirit asked me to do and I gave the message he put in my heart.

But that was NOT the end of it… It was only the beginning!!!

The Holy Spirit directed me to make a website, and so I did, it is at: www.TonyLamb.org

Then the Holy Spirit told me to start making youtube videos, so I did. In the youtube search box just type in [Tony Lamb] and you can find all my videos.

Then the Holy Spirit told me to start writing books, so I did.

Now keep in mind I am not a public speaker.

And I am not a videographer and I am not a writer, BUT I am what you say I am Lord.

Nothing more and nothing less.

I learned a very important lesson, a very hard lesson, and that is you can NOT argue with God, you lose before you even start.

As God will not accept a NO answer IF GOD WANTS YOU FOR A WORK.

CHAPTER TWO
Be Not Afraid Speak

A couple of months after I started to speak, Satan crawled up on my shoulder and spoke into my ear, he said:
You get invited to church and NOW you think you are Moses.

This kind of shocked me and I didn't know what to think so I quit speaking for a while. As this really shook me.

BUT then a couple months later, one Sunday early in the morning about 1:30 the Holy Spirit woke me up and told me to WRITE down a message. I turned on my light on my nightstand beside my bed and I grabbed a piece of paper and I began to write down what He gave me to write. It was ONLY 4 words.

I wrote it down and folded it and placed the note on my night stand. I turned off the light and quickly fell back asleep.

We went to Sunday School like we had done for a while and Brother Danny was the Sunday School teacher, and we listened intently and followed along in our Bible. Then all of a sudden without skipping a beat as part of the lesson he said: (BE NOT AFRAID SPEAK).

I thought; Did I really just hear that, from Brother Danny?   Was it a message from God, through Brother Danny?

BUT then, only about 5 minutes later he said it again a second time and again, without skipping a beat and as part of his lesson he said: (BE NOT AFRAID SPEAK). Then I knew that God had given me a message through Brother Danny.

On the way home I was explaining, excitedly, how I had gotten a message from God through Brother Danny and I don't think he even realized it, after all God had been dealing with my heart about SPEAKING AGAIN.

When I got home, I went straight to bed like I usually did after Sunday church for a nap.

The Holy Spirit woke me up about an hour later and reminded me I had a note from the Holy Spirit from 1:30 AM that morning and He prompted me to get up and read it.

I sat up, I found the folded note on my night stand, and when I opened the note I almost fainted and my knees began to knock, I was in awe, it was unbelievable, BUT THERE IT WAS STARING ME RIGHT IN THE FACE, my note from the Holy Spirit written by my own hand and the note read: BE NOT AFRAID, SPEAK.

But it gets even better, later that evening (for whatever reason, I felt compelled to do this) I started to thumb through the pages of my Bible and as the pages flew past my thumb, I stopped and without looking took my index finger and POINTED to a verse in the Bible and THAT verse was:

ACTS 18:9
THEN SPOKE THE LORD TO PAUL BY A NIGHT VISION, SPEAK HOLD NOT THY PEACE.

God is so amazing only if we let Him be.

I started to speak again, and today I offer to speak at almost any venue or church I am invited to speak at. I now do not fear public speaking, I consider it a privilege, and a honor to give my testimony so that others may be inspired and that my testimony might strengthen faith and lead people to give their hearts to Jesus.

As there is NO salvation or safety from what is to come except through Jesus Christ.

Deuteronomy 19: 15
at the mouth of two witnesses, or at the mouth of three witnesses, shall the matter be established.

How many people today are having Rapture dreams, Tribulation dreams, dreams of hell all manner of prophetic dreams are coming from all kinds of people believers and non-believers alike.

There are others with dreams & visions who are (or were) watchmen in the service of the Lord, like David Wilkerson, Dimetri Dudaman, Henry Gruver and many others. Youtube is covered up with people who have had prophetic dreams of the last days.

Believe the Bible, Bad times are coming and YOU need to prepare with Jesus Christ in your heart first. I know exactly what you are thinking: I'll buy food, water, water filters, guns, ammo, medical supplies and the like but your preps will not save you.

Remember: (At the mouth of two or three witnesses)

Only Jesus can save anyone from what is coming, so prepare with Jesus as He should be your very first prep.

I was commanded to: WAKE UP AND TELL THE PEOPLE.

And that is what I have attempted to do every day of my Christian walk.

DO NOT PLACE YOUR FAITH & TRUST IN A PREACHER, teacher, prophet, government, military, science, or any faith, religion, church and NOT EVEN ME, - ONLY place your faith & trust in Jesus Christ and in His word ONLY in the King James Bible.

CHAPTER THREE

A Word From God, For America

I have received a word from the Lord to give to you America.

Jeremiah 51:7
Babylon hath been a golden cup in the LORD's hand,

that made all the earth drunken:

the nations have drunken of her wine;

therefore the nations are mad.

Isaiah 13:9
Behold, the day of the Lord cometh, cruel both with wrath and fierce anger, to lay the land desolate: and he shall destroy the sinners there of out of it.

Isaiah 13: 13
Therefore I will shake the heavens, and the earth shall remove out of her place, in the wrath of the Lord of hosts and in the day of his fierce anger.

Isaiah 13:6
Howl ye: for the day of the Lord is at hand: it shall come as a destruction from the almighty.

Isaiah 25:19 & 20
The earth is utterly broken down, the earth is moved exceedingly.

The earth shall reel to and fro like a drunkard and shall be removed like a cottage: and the transgression thereof shall be heavy upon it: and it shall fall, and not rise again.

Isaiah 47:5
Sit thou silent and get thee into darkness, O daughter of the Chaldeans: For thou shalt no more be called the lady of kingdoms.

1 Thessalonians 5:3
For when they shall say, Peace and Safety: Then sudden destruction cometh upon them, As travail upon a woman with child: AND THEY SHALL NOT ESCAPE.

Isaiah 24: 5
The earth also is defiled under the inhabitants thereof: Because they have transgressed the law, changed the ordinances, broken the everlasting covenant.

Isaiah 24:6
Therefore hath the curse devoured the earth, and they that dwell therein are desolate: Therefore the inhabitants of the earth are burned: and few men left.

Isaiah 24: 1
Behold the Lord maketh the earth empty and maketh it waste, and turneth it upside down, and scattereth abroad the inhabitants thereof.

Isaiah 24:3
The land shall be utterly emptied, and utterly spoiled: For the Lord hath spoken this word.

Isaiah 24:19
The earth is utterly broken down, The earth is clean dissolved, the earth is moved exceedingly.

Isaiah 42:14
I have long time holden my peace: I have been still, and refrained myself: NOW will I cry like a travaling woman: I will destroy and devour at once.

Isaiah 46: 9 & 10

Remember former things of old: For I am God, and there is none else: I am God and there is none like me

Declaring the end from the beginning, AND I WILL DO ALL MY PLEASURE.

1 Peter 4:7

The end of all things is at hand: be ye therefore sober, and watch unto prayer.

Jeremiah 51:13

O thou that dwellest upon many waters, Abundant in treasures, thine end is come, and the measure of thy covetousness.

Jeremiah 32:27

Behold, I am the Lord, the God of all flesh, is there anything to hard for me?

Galatians 6:7

Be not deceived; God is not mocked: for whatsoever a man soweth, that shall he also reap.

Revelation 18:8
Therefore shall her plagues come in one day, death, and mourning, and famine; and she shall be utterly burned with fire: for strong is the Lord God who judgeth her.

Revelation 16: 8
And the fourth angel poured out his vial upon the sun; and power was given unto him to scorch men with fire.

Luke 12: 49
I am come to send fire on the earth; and what will I, if it be already kindled?

Zechariah 9: 4
Behold, the LORD will cast her out, and he will smite her power in the sea; and she shall be devoured with fire.

Matthew 13: 40
As therefore the tares are gathered and burned in the fire; so shall it be in the end of this world.

Matthew 13: 50
And shall cast them into the furnace of fire: there shall be wailing and gnashing of teeth.

Ezekiel 39:8
Behold it is come, and it is done, saith the Lord God: this is the day whereof I have spoken.

The Lord spoke to me lying in bed one night, He spoke in my heart and in my head, it was as if I could hear His voice. He told me to give you this:

America 'YOU' have been 'THAT' golden cup in my hand and I have blessed America like no other nation on earth.

YOU that dwell on many waters, you have the Atlantic Ocean to the east, the Pacific Ocean to your west, the Gulf of Mexico to the south and the Great Lakes to your north, 'who else do you think I am talking off'.

And who else has been so abundant in treasure as America.

And are not all the nations of the earth mad now?

My stiff-necked people instead of getting on your knees and repenting of your sins you have incurred my wrath, NOW my judgment comes.

I have holden my peace for a long time, BUT NO MORE.

Now you America will feel my wrath.

Another calamity comes soon upon you and much worse than before.

Surely you will see that it is, 'I who judgeth you'.

And surely you will fall to your knees and repent of your sins.

Or much worse is to come.

Woe to America!

Judgment Comes!

That is the end of my message I was given to give to the people.

Extreme weather, famine, war, power outages, pestilence, total economic collapse, no gas, no power, no food, earthquakes, volcanoes, tsunamis, nuclear attacks on American cities it is all coming and much worse is to come.

Even your gold and silver will become worthless see Ezekiel 7:19

I know these messages do not make me very popular, but like Jeremiah I was not called to tickle your ears. I was called to give you the truth, TO WARN THE PEOPLE. I will only tell you the truth.

Of what is coming and you can see it right in front of your face.

BUT also to remind you of salvation that is being offered to you by Jesus Christ.

He shed his precious blood for you and he freely gave up his life for you, so that you and I might be saved from what is about to come upon the whole earth BUT especially America.

As America was that golden cup in the Lord's hand.

And to whom much is given, much is expected.

NOW, not tomorrow, but right now you see what is coming and there is no escaping what is to come.

Only Jesus can save anyone from what is to come.

Humble yourself before Almighty God, Sincerely and humbly admit that you are a sinner and repent of all sin known and all sin unknown. Admit, recognize that Jesus is the son of God sent to this earth, who was crucified and died on an old wooden cross, for your sins and mine. And that He was buried but on the third day He arose from the grave and walked this earth again. And that he ascended up to heaven in sight of men. And now sits on the right hand of the Father.

Awaiting His glorious and triumphant return to Rapture His faithful home.

Humble yourself, repent of all your sins and beg and plead the blood of Jesus washes over you and washes all your sin away. Washes you clean, white as snow. Then beg Jesus to come into your heart to lead you, guide you and protect you all your days upon this earth.

Our time grows ever so short.

One day soon Jesus will return to Rapture His faithful away home and we will be with Jesus forevermore, that where He is, is where we shall be.

We pray we see you on the streets of gold one day very soon.

Remember the ONLY way to survive what is to come, IS TO NOT BE HERE, AS IN BEING RAPTURED.

Always remember that you are a precious child of the most high living God, who loves you and who treasures you above all the gold of the earth and above all the stars of heaven.

And we love and treasure you as well.

WITH MUCH LOVE & MORE GRACE FROM ABOVE

AMEN

CHAPTER FOUR
The Dreams Start

I have had so very many dreams and so many horrific dreams that it would be impossible for me to put every dream in chronological order. Also, I believe the Holy Spirit gave me these dreams but, in His wisdom, He then took many of them from me so as not to cause me to be so troubled by these dreams that I could not function.

I notice that now the Holy Spirit will bring these dreams back to me when He has a purpose in doing so.

And since the Holy Spirit directed me to write this book, I am asking and praying to the Holy Spirit to bring these forgotten dreams back so that I can write this book and glorify Jesus and His Holy Name.

So, I do this work NOT for me but for you Lord to warn the people as He commanded me to do.

Thy will be done.

In late Sept. 2017 I awoke from a horrific dream.

It was very horrific. I woke up gasping for air, choking on tears, and I crawled to the foot of my bed where I got on my knees and I sobbed uncontrollably.

I cried so hard I choked and gagged on my tears which flowed like water.

Through my sobbing I begged the Lord: 'WHY, WHY DID YOU SHOW ME SUCH SUFFERING AND PAIN, WHY DID YOU SHOW ME SOMETHING SO HORRIBLE, WHY LORD, - WHY'.

I PRAYED, I SOBBED, I CHOKED AND THE TEARS FELL LIKE RAIN.

I have no idea of how long I was on my knees praying and crying, but I stayed on my knees and I was determined to STAY ON MY KNEES until I got an answer.

WHY WAS I SHOWN SOMETHING SO HORRIFIC?

Through my tears I prayed on, determined to get some kind of an answer.

Now, I know God is no respecter of persons and that God will do all His pleasure.

God owes me nothing. God does NOT have to give me an answer.

But I just felt like there was something else, something more than just what I was shown.

There had to be a reason a why I was shown such horror.

So, I prayed on with tears streaming down my face I prayed on asking, begging for an explanation of WHY I was shown such a horrific dream. What did it all mean, why was I shown this dream, it was very graphic, in your face and it was up close and personal to me.

Finally, the Holy Spirit came to me and consoled me, wiped away my tears and He gave me an answer:

I LOVE YOU SO VERY MUCH, BUT I AM ABOUT TO CUT YOU OFF.

The Holy Spirit revealed to me that God was tired of being mocked, marginalized and ignored and God was about to pour out His wrath upon America.

The very same God who had blessed America so very much who made America powerful, and strong. Who made America the most prosperous nation ever on the face of the earth was about to remove the blessing and bring wrath to America.

Jeremiah 51: 7
Babylon hath been a golden cup in the LORD's hand, that made all the earth drunken: the nations have drunken of her wine; therefore the nations are mad.

The same God who judged the Jews (His chosen people) He judged them so very harsh was about to judge America even MORE HARSH.

Now I knew the meaning of my horrific dream, I knew why I was given this dream.

God has a meaning and a purpose in everything He does, God's words will not return void back to Him.

Every word, every dot, and every tittle has meaning in your King James Bible or it would NOT be there.

So, everything God does or says has meaning and purpose.

Yes, we are in the 'Time of Sorrows' and things are only going to get worse.

Everything gets worse. I see major complications from the vaxxine are already here. It will open up many horrors, complications and unwanted side effects and even death to the people who take this.

It seems several years ago there was a 'HIGH LEVEL' meeting in hell. All the top brass was there, all the big wigs in industry, technology, government, defense, along with the World Health Organization and even the CDC and many other government agencies were there. And you know many of their names and faces, but I will not go into that here.

The topic of discussion was: HOW TO MAKE EVERY PERSON ON EARTH WANT TO TAKE THE MARK OF THE BEAST, VOLUNTARILY, EVEN DEMAND IT.

As they all knew full well that to just INTRODUCE the Mark of the Beast, it would be rejected by Billions of people worldwide, even the fence sitting Christians and even the prosperity Christians, Mormons, the Seventh Day Adventist and even many non-Christians, all would refuse the Mark of the Beast.

So, the discussion was HOW to get everyone on board to: 'WANT and BEG for the Mark of the Beast?'

Many ideas were discussed, and it was finally decided that a world-wide pandemic was the best option.

They would make a vaxxine with so many bad side effects, that would kill more people than the virus. It would have many side effects, and would alter your DNA, include an operating system, HEK 293, Hydro-gel (nano robots in your blood altering your DNA, cutting out sections of your DNA code and replacing the gap with new code (Satan's code).

This vaxxine was designed to open the door for the Mark of the Beast.

With all the negative side effects and the many deaths attributed to this botched vaxxine after the Tribulation starts the Anti-Christ would offer us a way to be relieved from all the negative side effects, plus give us many benefits.

In other words, the antichrist offers you LIFE where the old vaxxine only offers you death. And that way the antichrist will be hailed as a savior of mankind. This is how the antichrist attains god status.

The 'Mark of the Beast' will save your life. (They will tell you).

The Satanists know full well that many will refuse the Mark of the Beast, but they will tell you that YOU already took the vaxxine and your DNA has already been altered and it's to late to turn back now. As the damage has already been done and the Mark of the Beast now will be your only salvation, your only way to live.

(IN FOR A PENNY, IN FOR A POUND).

Besides the Mark of the Beast will have many amazing benefits. You will be free from all common diseases, you will live forever, (so they will tell you). You will be smarter, faster, more energy, heal faster, live longer, and free from many ailments found in many people like high blood pressure, diabetes, heart disease, almost all your ailments will be cured by this Mark of the Beast. Just another reason why everyone will be demanding it. They will demand it to LIVE.

It's all a lie straight from the pit of hell.

Revelation 9: 6

And in those days shall men seek death, and shall not find it; and shall desire to die, and death shall flee from them.

IF you take the vaxxine (if you survive) you will have many very bad side effects and most of them will be life threatening.

This is all part of their Game Plan just to get you to beg for the Mark of the Beast. To demand the Mark of the Beast as a cure for the vaccine.

(The vaxxine is here) The Mark of the Beast is coming, but first we get Raptured, and then the Tribulation starts.

Then the antichrist is revealed and only then is his 'Mark of the Beast' revealed that will be promoted as a salvation to all mankind.

And then all HELL COMES TO EARTH.

PLEASE DO NOT TAKE THIS VAXXINE as that path only leads straight to hell and there is no turning back after you have altered your DNA.

I have prayed on this vaxxine many times and early on the Holy Spirit told me that the vaxxine was: AN ABOMINATION TO GOD.

And later the Holy Spirit told me that: the vaxxine was the gateway to hell.

I was also given this: If Jesus were alive today do you think H would take anything that would change His DNA?

(NO)

Then why should we?

Everyone knows that mRNA will changes your DNA, that is what it does.

And once you change your DNA you are no longer made in the image of God but are then made in the image of man or more correctly in the image of Satan.

In these last days God will reveal Himself as never before.

2 Timothy 1:7
For God has not given us the spirit of fear, but of power, and of love and of a sound mind.

God Bless you and God keep you and yours is our prayer.

WITH MUCH LOVE AND MORE GRACE FROM ABOVE

AMEN

CHAPTER FIVE

I Saw The Tribulation

I am just the dust of the earth and no one is beneath me, the only thing special about me is I am forgiven and I am God's dirt.

I was born and you were born for this time right now.

We are truly blessed to be alive in these last days to see the heavy hand of God at work. And in these last days God will reveal Himself as never before.

To see and be a part of the Rapture and to see the Time of Sorrows unfolding before us right now, we are truly blessed.

I was called for this time right now. I was dedicated to God before I was born. I was called a Last Days Watchman by God and given many dreams and visions for this time right now.

Almost all of my dreams were about the Tribulation, a few were about the Time of Sorrows, but it was never shown to me which was which.

If a dream were truly frightening and horrific, I would just assume it was in the Tribulation. And I was never shown any order in which these things occurred or given any time reference. All I knew was that IT was coming.

There is NO chronological order or time frame as no order was given to me.

Since all my prophetic dreams were given to me by the Holy Spirit AND I received confirmation for ALL of my significant dreams.

I am nothing, but the dust of the earth and I am NOT special in any way. God called me for a work and in that work I will be faithful.

Also, the Holy Spirit has come to me so many times I recognize His voice, he is never in disagreement with the word of God in the King James Bible and He is always respectful and in agreement with Jesus Christ.

So, I have no doubt what I tell you WILL come about, ONLY the order and timing of these events are in question.

I will attempt to place an order according to world events that are happening now. And expand from the very near future into the Tribulation.

And PLEASE keep in mind the Rapture is the Big Secret, as no one knows the Day or the Hour. But we are to know the season, and we are most definitely IN the Season. So the Rapture could happen at any time, any minute.

My personal opinion based upon Biblical examples and what I was shown is that the Rapture will occur JUST before a VERY MAJOR CATASTROPHIC EVENT TAKES PLACE.

So, yes we, faithful Christians may see and feel some calamities to come, but we MUST remain faithful and true as God's word and God's promises will be fulfilled.

So, no matter what comes, no matter what we see and feel we MUST remain faithful and True to God as there is NO other way to get to heaven only by faith, trust in God and to BELIEVE.

According to my dreams and what is happening in the world we are about to experience a catastrophic economic collapse. Everything paper collapses, real estate, bonds, stocks, EVERYTHING PAPER COLLAPSES, and eventually even gold and silver will become worthless.

Ezekiel 7:19 They shall cast their silver in the streets, and their gold shall be removed: their silver and their gold shall not be able to deliver them in the day of the wrath of the Lord: they shall not satisfy their souls, neither fill their bowels: because it is the stumblingblock of their iniquity.

This collapse will hit America especially hard since America owes so much to so many.

FEMA Camps are coming and people will go in but no one leaves. At first this will be for everyone who is homeless, and there will be a LOT of homeless people.

In one of my dreams, I saw millions of Americans lining the ditches leading out of towns all across America, as they were all evicted from their homes. Most of these ended up in FEMA Camps.

War is coming to America. I saw foreign troops with blue helmets in America first.

Then I saw Russian and Chinese troops in America after that and they killed many.

I saw nuclear weapons going off over several American cities.

Jeremiah 50:23 How is the hammer of the whole earth cut asunder and broken! How is Babylon become a desolation among nations!

I saw America go dark, cold and silent. As in like an EMP weapon is detonated high above America and America goes dark, cold and deathly silent from coast to coast.

Isaiah 47:5 Sit thou silent and get thee into darkness, O daughter of the Chaldeans: For thou shalt no more be called the lady of kingdoms.

I saw much famine upon the land, it seemed as if everyone was hungry. There was NO food to be had at any price. And the people resorted to eating rats, wild animals, bark, leaves, grass and final they resorted to eating people and this became very common and acceptable among the people.

In the Tribulation BILLIONS will die, about 3 ½ Billion will die in just the first half of the Tribulation and nearly that many in the second half of the Tribulation.

God sends His wrath and Satan sends his wrath and the people will be caught in the middle. This earth will be NO PLACE TO BE.

And as I said before fallen angels will walk the earth and destroy 1/3 of mankind. The Bible says this NOT ME in Revelation 9: 14 & 15.

I saw billions of demons released upon the earth, making the people do unspeakable things to other people and animals.

All manner of disease and pestilence will come upon the earth, some made by nature and some made by man.

Asteroid strikes, Earthquakes, volcanoes, Tsunamis it is all coming, that and much worse. Have you noticed that everything is speeding up and the intensity and frequency of these calamities is increasing?

WELL, it will continue to increase and these natural disasters will take many lives.

This is the time of 'Birth Pains' and just like birth pains our calamities will increase with intensity and frequency UINTIL the Rapture comes and Jesus removes His faithful remnant from this dying world.

AND IT IS DYING.

I saw a massive wall of water come ashore on the east coast, and on the west coast destroying everything in its path.

Jeremiah 51:42
The sea is come upon Babylon: she is covered with the multitude of the waves thereof.

I have had so many dreams of death and destruction.

I saw people sitting around a campfire on a lake shore cutting meat from a body to cook and eat.

I saw parents walking down a flight of stairs holding their precious baby in their arms lovingly. They walked into the kitchen and placed the baby in a large pot of water on the stove and they turned the burner on. (In that dream I never heard the baby or saw it move, so I have no idea if it was dead or alive)

I saw parents sell their children for a hand full of rice or beans to strangers at their front door. Knowing full well they would be sold into the child sex slave market or that they were to be eaten.

Jeremiah 19:9 And I will cause them to eat the flesh of their sons and the flesh of their daughters: and they shall eat everyone the flesh of his friend in the

siege and straightness wherewith their enemies and they that seek their lives, shall straighten them.

The earth shall reel to and fro and stagger and shudder like a drunkard.

I saw the sun go crazy with strong heat and much radiation and cause sores upon the people and cause many to have cataracts and go blind. And the sun burned many people, most crops, fields, grass, trees were destroyed and many people died because of the great heat.

Many rivers, streams and lakes dried up. And the little water left was not drinkable and to do so would cause an excruciating long drawn-out death.

Revelation 18:18
Therefore shall her plagues come in one day, death, and mourning and famine, and she shall be utterly burned with fire: for strong is the Lord God who judges her.

Isaiah 24:6
Therefore hath the curse devoured the earth, and they that dwell therein are desolate: therefore the inhabitants of the earth are burned: and few men left.

People will seem to go mad.

Nature will turn against man.

Even family will turn against their own family.

2 Timothy 3:1 through 5
This know also that in the last days perilous times shall come.

For men shall be lovers of their own selves, covetous, boasters, proud, blasphemers, disobedient to parents, unthankful, unholy.

Without natural affection, incontinent, fierce, despisers of those that are good.

Traitors, heady, high-minded, lovers of pleasure more than lovers of God.

Having a form of godliness, but denying the power thereof: from such turn away.

There is more written about this period than any other time, including when Jesus walked the earth.

So, God wants you to know what is coming.

This is what Jesus says about this time:

Matthew 24:21
For then shall be great tribulation, such as was not since the beginning of the world, to this time, NO, nor ever shall be.

And like God made a way for Noah and his family to survive the great flood, and Lot and his family to survive the destruction of Sodom.

God has provided a way for those faithful to Jesus Christ and His word in the King James Bible to escape the judgment to come upon the whole earth.

And that way is to be faithful to Jesus now, and NOT after the Rapture because IF you miss the Rapture, you will find yourself in the Tribulation.

If you are not saved, washed in the blood of Jesus and born again or luke-warm or one who attends an apostate church.

You need to humble yourself before God, and repent of your sins, plead the blood of Jesus wash over you and wash all your sins away.

Beg Jesus to come into your heart and give you a new heart.

As there is no other way to escape what is coming EXCEPT TO NOT BE HERE.

As in being Raptured.

Remember Jesus paid the price for your redemption with His own blood and His very life.

All you must do is repent of sin and ask Jesus into your heart to lead and guide you every day.

I am sorry IF this book offends anyone as that was not my intention, BUT it is my intention to WAKE UP THE PEOPLE as to what is coming right at them and soon.

We are NOT promised tomorrow.

In these last days NOW is not the time to deny Jesus in any way.

SO, please carry your King James Bible everywhere you can.

And please say the blessing over every meal you eat.

And repent of sin every time you pray.

Because these days Satan is in everything.

I tell you so very many churches are in apostacy it is almost impossible to find a good full King James Bible teaching church any more.

You are more likely to find God at a small independent church or a home church than in any organized church.

So please be aware of false churches, false teachers and preachers who will tickle your ears BUT drag you to hell with them.

DO NOT follow a faith, religion, a man or woman (NOT EVEN ME) BUT follow the ONLY one who can save you from this dying world, and that one is Jesus Christ and His word in the King James Bible.

Always remember that YOU are a precious child of the Most High Living God, who loves you and who treasures YOU above all the gold of the earth and above all the stars of heaven.

And we love and treasure you as well.

God Bless you and yours MIGHTILY

WITH MUCH LOVE AND MORE GRACE FROM ABOVE

AMEN

CHAPTER SIX

Two Tribulation Dreams; A Foggy Day and a Red Truck

In this dream I was like a fly on a street light on a corner in a city. No one saw me, it was like I was not there physically but I was there in spirit and I saw and heard everything.

At first, I didn't know what to think of this dream it seemed so disconnected, fragmented, surreal, as if it was in a fog.
The more I thought about the dream the more I realized that it was a two-part dream.

I was at an intersection that had a red light. Looking down the street in front of me were houses with neatly trimmed front lawns.

To my right, I saw what looked like more homes and to my left through the intersection I saw what looked like small businesses, I looked behind me and I saw apartments and what looked like townhouses. This was a very neat upscale looking neighborhood.

I did not see any sun, it was a very dreary day, kind of hazy or in a fog, it was not night time but it was hazy outside for being daytime.

The next thing I saw was the light had changed, it turned red. But then I saw a red pick-up truck came barreling through the red light, then it swerved and crashed into a parked car. People rushed to see who was in the truck and to see if they could help.

But when they peered into the truck, they were amazed to find no one in the truck.

And right when that happened there were tires screeching from all over the city and you could hear crashes going on all over. Then I saw what I think was a jet airplane crash in a field about a mile away in a terrific fireball and many people screamed and wept.

Then I heard blood curdling screams and shrieks of sheer terror coming from the homes, the odd thing was this all started at the exact same time that the red truck ran the red light and crashed.

I somehow was able to see inside of some of the homes and I saw parents frantically searching for their missing children and babies, looking in beds, in cribs, under beds, in closets, in cabinets. They were searching for their missing children and they were in a panic and screaming in terror.

Then I saw lots of people were running around outside and they were crying and weeping and running to and fro. They were desperately searching for their missing children. They were looking under parked cars, in bushes, knocking on neighbor's doors in a panic.

They were looking for their children and babies who had mysteriously vanished in the blink of an eye and sometimes right in front of them.

The people were weeping, wailing and gnashing their teeth in anguish looking for their children.

But this was not a local event this was happening worldwide everywhere at the exact same time.

The people were crying and praying in a language I could not understand. They seemed to be for the most part looking up terrified and begging and crying out for forgiveness and they were weeping and speaking in a language that had no meaning to me.

You can tell by their face they were terrified that they could not find their babies and children, they were in a panic and their eyes were filled with terror for their missing children.

But not everyone was crying and praying there were a lot of people who were just standing around and looking with a puzzled look on their face.
A look I can only describe as a 'Deer in the Headlights Look'.

They were just dumfounded and had a kind of numb look on their faces. A kind of 'What Just Happened Look'.

Many people seemed to be in a panic, crying and running to and fro as they were looking for their children who were lost or missing. It seemed like everyone was looking for someone.

There were some people who were standing outside shaking their fist up at heaven with a very mad even enraged look on their face, and they were very upset and they were speaking very upset with a look of rage on their face. They were speaking in a language that I could not understand but you just knew that they were cursing God for what just happened.

Then this foggy dream seemed to close and go dark. But in only a moment I started a new dream.

The second part of my dream was somewhat similar in that there was not any fog this time but now there was smoke everywhere, and the dream again was surreal as in a fog from the smoke.

I seemed to be on the very same street corner again.

This time you could not recognize the same scene, I just knew it was the exact same scene from my previous dream.

But this time there were few people and this time they were cursing (I think) as again they were speaking in a language I could not understand.

But you can tell by the look on someone's face when they are really mad and shaking their fist up toward Heaven, you get an idea of what they are saying even if you don't understand the words.

I just knew this was the same scene as before, this time all the houses, all of the buildings had fallen down and were in burning heaps on the ground, all the trees, grass and crops were all burned up with fire There were few people, but what people there were, they were running about screaming and shaking there fist up at Heaven, at God and cursing God for allowing this to happen to them.

The people were in tattered clothes, malnourished, un-kept, unclean, filthy, in rags with sores all over them and they looked as if they had not bathed in years, and they were screaming and cursing God.

There are 3 kinds of people in the world,

Those going to Hell and don't care and curse God.

Those who are going to be Raptured before the Tribulation starts.

And those who are Luke Warm, and they know about salvation and the saving grace of Jesus Christ, but are NOT in the Will and Grace of God.

This group knows the truth, as they go to church or have gone to Church, they know the truth but they were NOT in God's will. They were NOT following the word of God or twisting the Bible to fit their needs.

This group was following a doctrine of demons straight to hell and this group was on their knees.

This group will be crying and whaling and repenting after the rapture but to no avail as it THEN will be too late.

Now this Luke Warm group will have to endure the Tribulation, and NOT take the mark of the Beast, not worship the beast, not worship his image, his mark or his number and NEVER deny Jesus Christ to be able to enter the Kingdom of Heaven.

This group knows that NOW, the only way to attain heaven is to be martyred for their faith and their testimony of Jesus Christ.

They attended a feel good, prosperity church that never had a call for repentance of sin, never talked about the wrath of God, sin, Revelation, the Tribulation, Time of Sorrows, nothing bad only the feel-good parts of the Bible.

But they were deceived because no matter how good you think you are, no matter how many good works you do, IF you do not repent of your sin and invite Jesus into your heart as your Lord and savior you will still go to hell.

Because all your good works are as dung before God, without repentance of sin. And without believing that Jesus is the Son of God who died for you and for me, who was buried and on the third day arose from the grave.

It's so simple – pray up and be in the will of God, be pleasing to God. Humble yourself to God and repent of your sins, and invite Jesus to enter into your heart as your Lord and savior, in Jesus name. And BELIEVE in Jesus Christ.

As Jesus is the truth, the life and the way. And only through Jesus can you, me or anyone be saved.

It's a simple choice but it's the MOST important choice you will EVER make in your life.

God on numerous occasions has shown me the Tribulation through dreams and visions and what I have been shown is literally Hell on Earth from beginning to end and many Billions will die.

As the door on Noah's Ark was closed by God, this door to the Age of Grace also will be closed by God, and like the people who missed getting on the Ark, the Bible says, the rain came and washed them all away.

DO NOT get left behind and washed away by the coming flood.

Right now, the door to salvation is open, BUT not for much longer.

One day soon God will close that door, as the Rapture WILL HAPPEN and once God closes that door it will never be reopened again.

And then you will enter the Tribulation.

We pray for you, that you are NOT left behind, that you enter into the Ark, and come into the safety and salvation of Jesus Christ.

Have you been watching the news? Banks are closing right now, economic collapse is coming, Famine is coming, earthquakes are coming, volcanoes, Tsunamis are coming, war is coming, more severe pestilence is coming. Now they talk about these things on the nightly news: SO, YOU KNOW IT'S COMING

I warned several years ago that we were entering the Time of Sorrows and things were only going to get worse and worse.

DID I LIE?

NOW is the last call to get into the saving grace of Jesus Christ. As we are that close to the Rapture.

Time is very short and YOU do not want to miss the 'Boat' the Rapture.

Because IT is coming and there is NOTHING, I can do but warn you and that is exactly what I have been attempting to do since 2014.

I am NOT affiliated with any church as they would not have me. (And I consider that a badge of honor).

I was actually asked by my last pastor TO NOT associate his church or his name with anything I did, printed or spoken. Yes, I was banned from speaking at my last church.

I was asked to NOT come to the altar during altar call as my getting on my knees was too distracting to the rest of the service.

I was banned from speaking ill of all these fake bibles who delete the word God an average of 66 times (interesting number), they delete the word Jesus an average of 44 times, they delete the mention of the word of the blood of Jesus and without the blood of Jesus there is no atoning for sin. And they totally delete the word sodomite from most of these (so called modern bibles) I see these fake bibles as the work of Satan to change the word of God as you change or delete words you change the meaning of the word of God. And that was why I was banned for speaking against these fake bibles.

And this and other reasons is why I say, I DID NOT LEAVE, MY CHURCH LEFT ME.

WHAT WOULD JESUS SAY? To forgive and to pray for them.

DO not FOLLOW A RELIGION, A PERSON, A FAITH and I ask people to not even follow me, BUT follow only HIM that can save you, me or anyone from what is to come and that ONE would be Jesus Christ, Him and His word in the King James Bible ONLY.

As it's NOT a religion or a faith and NOT even a pastor that will get you to heaven, but it is a repentant heart, forgiveness toward others for transgressions against you, a humble heart, a willing, kind, loving heart with a childlike faith and BELIEVING in Jesus Christ that will get you to heaven.

My prayer is that SOMEONE, somewhere who reads this will get on their knees and cry out to God and repent of sin and invite Jesus into their heart as their Lord and savior.

IF I can save just ONE person from hell then ALL I have done will not have been in vain.

Just one Lord, JUST ONE.

Remember these are the Last Days, and we should NOT deny Jesus in any way. So please carry your Bible everywhere you can and say the blessing over every meal and repent of sin every time you pray as today sin is in everything.

God Bless you, God keep you and may God's face shine down upon you and give you PEACE.

And we will look for you on the streets of gold one day very soon.

We pray for you and your family.

WITH MUCH LOVE AND MORE GRACE FROM ABOVE

AMEN

CHAPTER SEVEN

Billions of Demons and Four Fallen Angels Released Upon the Earth

June 12, 2017, I had a very vivid and compelling dream.
In my dream, I was standing in a field and an Angel came to me and said: 'Follow Me'. The Angel took me by the hand and we immediately shot up higher and higher, we went way past the clouds, we went so high the earth looked like a globe spinning below us.

But I was not afraid, I was calm and at peace with this angel holding my hand high above the earth. The earth was slowly turning below us and when the middle east came into view the angel then started descending very fast, then the angle crashed into the earth and we went underground. We must have gone maybe a mile underground maybe more or maybe a little less as I had no frame of reference. And all the while this angel was holding my hand, I was at peace and not afraid.

Then this angel stopped and he showed me all these caves running in all directions. There seemed to be miles and miles of caves running everywhere. And every cave was lined with billions of empty jail cells. Every cell I saw was empty and every jail door for every cell was sprung wide open.

I asked what is this? Then I was told that these cells held the demons that had been released upon the earth in the Last Days and especially the Tribulation.

Then I was shown these four beasts, but more correctly they were Fallen Angels and these were chained to the walls and they were NOT in jail cells. I was shown one particular beast and I was told he was the leader but he would not turn and look at me.

Then I became aware that to look into the eyes of this beast was instant death to anyone who looked into its eyes.

Now, I don't know, but maybe that is another reason why this beast did not turn and look at me, anyway I was thankful that that he did not look at me, because I DID NOT want to look into the eyes of this beast.

I was not afraid of this beast, not with this angel beside me and still holding my hand. None of these beasts stood up so I don't know how tall they were. They were all lying down and curled up, but still they were huge. And when they took a breath, you could hear a lot of air moving in and out of the beasts, with each breath they took. They were very muscular and they were huge even with them curled up and chained to the walls. I was told these 4 angels would be released upon the earth during the Tribulation and they would be responsible for destroying a third of mankind.

I felt a rage, a pure hatred and evil in these beasts, they hated God and everything of God, but they could not touch God so their rage was focused on what God loved - US.

We think we know anger and rage but our rage is nothing compared to the anger and rage of these beasts. They were filled with rage and you could feel it emitting from these beasts.

You could just feel they were just waiting for their time to be released upon the earth.

A rage beyond understanding or comprehension because God loved us above them. We were just frail humans, no powers, and we came along last. So, their logic was How Could God Love Us Above Them?

SOON, VERY SOON AND THEY KNEW THEY WOULD BE RELEASED UPON THE EARTH FOR THEIR SEASON OF DESTRUCTION.

Then I woke up and I prayed.

Then I was shown the following scripture.

Revelation 9:14 and 15
14 Saying to the sixth Angel which had the trumpet, loose the four angels which are bound in the great river Euphrates

15 And the four angels were loosed, which were prepared for an hour, and a day, and a month, and a year for to slay the third part of men.

But what of the Billions of demons released upon the earth?

The Holy Spirit just recently revealed to me what I am now about to tell you.

Have you seen the videos of people on that drug called FLAKKA? That is how many will act being possessed in the Tribulation.

Also, these demons will make their hosts do unspeakable things like eating people and animals alive and dead.

Women possessed will bend over in public in short skirts and exposing themselves, and offering themselves up to everyone to see or for anyone to 'use them' carnally, in public, in broad daylight anywhere and everywhere. The demons who possessed them made them offer themselves up for all to see and to use.

No one asked, they just took it as an invitation to use them and they were used by many men and even some women.

Remember why the fallen angels fell in the first place?

They had a very strong sex drive and most demons have a very strong sex drive as well. But in the Tribulation the nastiest and the worst demons will be released upon the earth and they will use humans for sexual purposes and for any and all purposes.

Revelation 6:2 & 4

That the sons of God saw the daughters of men that they were fair; and they took them wives of all which they chose.

There were giants in the earth in those days; and also after that, when the sons of God came into the daughters of men, and they bare children to them, the same became mighty men which were of old, men of renown.

These entities have an overpowering drive for sex and when they possess anyone, they start driving the host to do unspeakable things sexually.

There are examples of this throughout the world right now BUT it will get much, much worse the closer we get to the Tribulation. And this will explode in the Tribulation.

And NO not everyone will do this. But as we get close to the Tribulation this phenomenon will increase dramatically, and it has already started. I have read reports of this now happening in the world.

There are videos of women in crowds of people in public indoors and outdoors bending over and offering themselves up to anyone to use sexually. (Proof of demonic possession).

IF you are not saved, born again and washed in the precious blood of Jesus Christ, this you will be faced with or be a part of.

I am very sorry if this offends you but the Holy Spirit told me it was time to release this at this very late hour so that the people know what is coming.

But Much Worse is Coming.

The Rapture is so very soon, at one time I counted days, NOW I count hours.

Now is the time to humble yourself in sincere prayer and REPENT OF SIN.

Because there is NO surviving the horror, death and destruction to come –
EXCEPT TO NOT BE HERE.

As in being Raptured.

YES, God is merciful, loving and kind as He made a way for His faithful (to NOT
be here) and to NOT have to endure the death, destruction and all the horrors of the
Tribulation.

God always makes a way for His faithful, His remnant to escape HIS wrath. And
the Rapture is our rescue from what is to come upon this dying world.

But God is a God of rules, laws and God cannot break His own rules.

I said several years ago it was only going to get worse and worse. Well things are
still only going to get worse. But after the Rapture God lifts fully his hand of
protection and for the people left behind, they will see HELL ON EARTH.

God Bless you and God keep you and yours safe

AMEN

CHAPTER EIGHT

My Second Fallen Angel Dream, A Third of Mankind Destroyed

I had a dream and it was my second dream involving Fallen Angels. In this dream I saw several Fallen Angels and they were walking on the earth and they were destroying EVERYTHING in their path. I did not see how they were doing this, but they were destroying everything made by man and especially the people.

Now some might think they had like rays coming out of their finger tips or fire coming out of their mouths or eyes. I did not see any such thing. What I saw was a path of destruction about 1/3 or ¼ mile wide where they literally scorched the earth behind them.

They could not fly, they walked for this destruction.

And they destroyed people with rigor, not pausing to take a break, not sleeping, not getting tired, but destroying everything and everyone, day and night 24 hours a day, 7 days a week, never stopping and never slowing down.

They destroyed the very young and the very old it made no difference to them. They took no pity on men, women, children even babies. They destroyed everything and everyone as they knew their time was short for their season of destruction. So, they worked at a feverish pace day and night. Because they knew they had but a little time to work.

What I did see was, homes, stores, office buildings, all of it literally explode, like when a building has a gas leak and the building just explodes into ball of flames and a million pieces.

They were walking and destroying EVERYTHING in their path. People were cowering in homes and many people were running terrified screaming everywhere and no weapon could harm these fallen angels, and they knew it.

These Fallen Angels were big, huge and from a distance they looked to be 20 to 30 feet tall and as they got closer, they got bigger until they looked to be 40 to 50 feet tall when they got close to you.

These beasts were full of rage against mankind. Their rage was actually against God but they knew that they could never not touch God, so their rage was focused on the people, whom God had loved above them and the very thought of that filled them with a rage.

I saw the eyes of one of these beasts and their eyes were full of hate and rage and glowed red as fire embers glow. And again, I was reminded that to stare at the eyes of their leader was instant death. So, I took it the beast I was observing was not the leader.

Revelation 9:14 and 15
14 Saying to the sixth Angel which had the trumpet, loose the four angels which are bound in the great river Euphrates

15 And the four angels were loosed, which were prepared for an hour, and a day, and a month, and a year for to slay the third part of men.

I know I just showed these verses BUT they belong here as well.

The Euphrates River has now all but dried up and now these fallen angels are awake and moving and making animal noises that no earthly animal can make and you hear them rattling their chains and moaning.

THEY KNOW that they are about to be released for their season of destruction upon the earth. And they grow anxious to begin their work. Right now, there are numerous videos showing the Euphrates River running dry, and in the cracks and crevasses of the dry river bed they are recording all these sounds that these four beasts make in anticipation of being released upon the earth.

Revelation 16: 12

And the sixth angel poured out his vial upon the great river Euphrates; and the water thereof was dried up, that the way of the kings of the east might be prepared.

Then it went black in my dream, and when I reemerged what I saw then, I was in a different situation. I was under a house, under the floor in the crawl space between the floor and the ground and I was there with 3 or 4 other men and they were all scrambling frantically looking for something, anything to dig with.

They were looking for soup cans, a piece of wood anything to dig with as they were frantically digging holes to bury themselves in, (under the house). They did this to hide from the fallen angels before they got there and destroyed the house, they were under.

I remember thinking that their safety was NOT in burying themselves, their safety was in Jesus Christ, they were looking for the wrong kind of safety or salvation. I remember trying to talk to them about Jesus but no one looked at me, no one listened, they just kept frantically digging holes to bury themselves in.

I then realized, I was with them in spirit and they could not see me or hear me.

Demons and Fallen Angels will be released upon the world one-day, just like it says in the Bible and people will run frantic and hide themselves in the rocks and dens of the mountains.

I don't know when but I do know it is coming upon the earth during the Tribulation.

I remember hearing the term 'bad aliens' it was as if I heard a news cast and the radio was talking about them destroying everything before them, and to run or take cover. I never saw a radio, it was as if I heard the news cast from somewhere, and it was about these fallen angels.

So, if there are 'bad aliens' there must be 'good aliens' as well, right? And people think the 'good aliens' are here to help us. It is all a lie, and they are all demons from the pit of hell sent here to deceive and to destroy.

BUT, we who are faithful and true to Jesus Christ and in His will and grace and who are Pleasing to God, will be Raptured out of here before any of that comes to pass. Just another good reason to NOT be here. To live for Jesus NOW and skip the Tribulation that is bearing down on us and is soon to come.

The time to live for Jesus is NOW and NOT during the Tribulation, as you will have a very hard time to live for Jesus during the Tribulation, and you and your family will probably have to suffer greatly. And you probably will have your head removed for your faith and testimony of Jesus as it says in the Bible; 'and I saw the souls of them that were beheaded for the witness of Jesus, and for the word of God,'.

So if you insist on going that route, Good luck, as you will need it!
It's time to get right with God NOW, right NOW as a minute from now may be a minute to late.

I pray for all of you that you come to know the saving grace of Jesus Christ before it's too late.   God Bless you and God keep you and yours safe.

CHAPTER NINE

At the mouth of two witnesses

THE Bible, David Wilkerson, Dumitru Duduman, Henery Gruver, many others and me

Luke 21: 25
There will be signs in the sun, the moon and in the stars.

How many people missed the signs in the heavens? You know the blood moons, the eclipse, the Revelation 12 sign, and even signs in our sun, the moon, the stars and signs in the heavens?

How many people are missing the signs in the earth? You know: earthquakes, volcanoes, tsunamis, famine, war, pestilence, bank failures and economic collapse and so much more.

Acts 2: 19
And I will shew wonders in heaven above, and signs in the earth beneath; blood, and fire and vapor of smoke.

(I give you the Bible as the first witness)

There was a man named Pastor David Wilkerson who founded Teen Challenge and wrote several books, which his most popular book was 'THE CROSS AND THE SWITCHBLADE'.

In 1973 he had a vision of America being destroyed by 3 major earthquakes. These earthquakes started with the Cascadia fault running from Northern Calif. To Vancouver BC Canada.

That earthquake caused the San Andrea's fault to rupture. He did not name the Cascadia fault by name, as at that time it was unknown.

He called it a 'major earthquake in an area that was not known to be seismically active'. The Cascadia fault was only discovered about 20 years ago.

And the Cascadia fault is a sleeping monster, it has the potential to produce America's only 9.4 earthquake. But there is more, as that fault is a mega thrust fault and it is off shore which will also create a monster Tsunami from 100 to 300 feet high that will hit the West coast.

Scientist say everything west of I-5, will be destroyed including Seattle, Portland, Tacoma all the way down to San Diego and much more.

These earthquakes devastated the entire West Coast in his vision. But his vision didn't stop there, it went on to show him how those earthquakes would cause the New Madrid fault to rupture.

This earthquake would destroy much of the center of America.

Also, he saw a major bank in Europe, probably in Germany collapse, and bring the world including America into a serious depression, unlike anything the world has ever seen before.

Right now, Credit Suisse is on the very edge of collapse and also Deutsche Bank is as well teetering on the edge of collapse. We already have our banking problems with three banks collapsing in three days here in America and the FED is scrambling to contain that situation. Like the Dutch Boy with his finger in the dike. Soon they will run out of fingers and toes.

But when either one of these two European Banks collapse there will be nothing they can do, and THEN the entire world's economy will collapse in a scenario that will be many magnitudes worse that the 1929 crash.

BUT it will not be ONE of those banks, it will be both banks along with many other banks in Europe, America and all over the world.
As it's ALL COMING DOWN AND SOON!

All commerce would stop, money would become worthless paper. No stores would be open and even if they did open, they would have nothing to sell. And no way to run any debit or credit cards and at that point the cards or cash would be worthless.

David Wilkerson saw Americans suffer tremendously unlike ever before. And I saw this also.

(I give you the vision of Pastor David Wilkerson as the second witness).

I also have had dreams where major earthquakes devastated the West Coast from Canada all the way to San Diego. What I saw was almost every building was destroyed for a hundreds of miles from the earthquake.

Also, I saw a major Tsunami crash ashore on the West Coast, and what the earthquake didn't destroy the Tsunami washed away. Horrific devastation, such unimaginable pain and suffering is what I saw.

I have seen (in a dream) a major earthquake, destroy the entire West Coast the bay area, all the way down to the greater Los Angeles area, along with a Tsunami destroying what was left of the Oregon and Washington Coastal area and up to 100 miles inland in many areas.

I have had dreams where an economic collapse destroyed the world's economy but for some reason it hit America especially hard. Probably because we owe so very much money to everyone.

I saw people walking down a street, and money was blowing down the street and people would not even bend over to pick it up because it was worthless paper.

I saw America in the dark without electricity. Then I saw war in America. It seemed that everyone everywhere was fighting, rioting, looting, burning and killing.

Deuteronomy 19: 15
At the mouth of 2 witnesses or at the mouth of 3 witnesses shall a matter be established

Are my dreams lining up with David Wilkerson's visions a coincidence? I don't think so. (There are no coincidences when it comes to God).

David Wilkerson did as God commanded him to do, he wrote books about his vision. He preached and talked about his vision for America, but in 1974 America was doing great and didn't want to hear about doom and gloom.

So, many churches banned him from speaking. He paid a price for following what God told him to do. But he was true to God. Pastor Wilkerson passed away in April 2011.

(I give you my dreams as the third witness, (but there is more).

Luke 21: 11
And great earthquakes shall be in divers places, and famines, and pestilences, and fearful sights and great signs shall there be from heaven.

Today there are so many earthquakes in Southern California and in the Cascadia rift area scientist say the Big One is primed, loaded, past due and ready any minute to let loose with a monster earthquake

A 9.0 or greater that will destroy the whole West Coast. Remember it was not that long ago that California Had a 6.4 followed by a 7.1 earthquake? Scientist say it's just getting primed for the Big One, which just proves (it is coming and soon). I saw an article recently that stated: 'Since July 4th Southern California and the Cascadia area have had over 3000 earthquakes' this was published in 2022.

In 2022 a federal agency sent a team of scientist to study the Cascadia fault. This team was supposed to be there for about 7 days, but after only 2 days the team of scientist rushed their research and then requested to be evacuated because they felt their lives were in imminent danger. This is how serious and how close we are to the Cascadia fault rupturing and rupturing in a VERY BIG way.

Also is it just coincidence that Deutsche Bank (the Largest Bank in Germany) announced the layoff of 18,000 employees and the closing of many overseas operations, with more to come.

Deutsche Bank has been in serious trouble many years but now insiders say it's only a matter of time before the bank closes its doors for good.

This information comes directly from news articles: And here is the problem with Deutsche Bank it holds about 49 trillion dollars in derivatives which will all come due when the bank collapses.

These derivatives will then fall back on other banks in Europe, and they will collapse, then they will fall back onto other major banks throughout the world which holds notes, bonds or (loans) made to Deutsche Bank as well as some of their derivatives and then they will collapse.

Central Banks will collapse throughout the entire world, as no one can pay the 49 trillion dollar bill owed by Deutsche bank. Banks everywhere will collapse. All banks will close (for a while until a new digital currency can be instituted. But then people's confidence in fiat currency will collapse as well.

The total amount due to derivative holders (which the banks will owe) worldwide is estimated at over 2 Quadrillion dollars.

Where is that money coming from?

And now Credit Suisse is in the news a lot and that bank is teetering on the edge of collapse, as of 3-11-2023 America has now had three major banks collapse (with more to come).

And now they say over 200 American banks are in danger of collapse, more, much more is coming. This is how you bring down the entire world economically.

Our economic house of cards is about to totally collapse. And still the people refuse to see that we are just now entering a total collapse and a greater Depression than even 1929.

 Pestilences, I guess the new flesh-eating bacteria that is now running wild on the Gulf Coast could be considered a new Pestilence. This is just unfolding and appears to be a very serious situation.

Now every month there is a NEW strain of Covid that is ravaging the planet right now some are mild and some are very deadly.

There will be many new strains of disease some man made and some made by nature. This is coming also.

So now I give you the scientist as a fourth witness, do you need more?

Matthew 16: 3
And in the morning , it will be foul weather today: for the sky is red and lowering.   O ye hypocrites, ye can discern the face of the sky; but can not discern the signs of the times.

TO WHOM MUCH IS GIVEN MUCH IS EXPECTED.

America has been given a lot and America has sinned so very much.

(There have been people all over the earth who have had dreams and visions of a massive earthquake and tsunamis hitting the West Coast and even the east coast of America).

Keep watching and stay in prayer for that Blessed Hope, the Great Catching Away will take us home soon.

May God keep you and yours in His loving arms just like He held me, as there is NO safer place to be in these troubled times.

The only safe place to be.

Is with Jesus.

CHAPTER TEN

MY EARTHQUAKE DREAM

I had a dream on April 25, 2018. I was on a big hill covered in tall grass without any trees on the hill.

In every direction I was looking downhill.

When I looked, I saw homes, businesses, farms, industry, shopping centers, apartment buildings all around me at some distance from me.

I was standing at the top of this very large and tall grass covered hill and it was peaceful and very calm, and it was a very nice day warm, and the sun was shining.

The next thing I knew the ground started shaking so violently I could not stand and I fell to the ground and the shaking continued for several minutes.

This shaking seemed to last forever, and was so very strong that it shook everything down to the ground. Even though I lived in California for a number of years, I have never experienced an earthquake. So, I have no way to gauge the strength of this earthquake. To me is seemed to be very violent and exceedingly strong and it seemed to go on forever.

Finally, the shaking stopped, and then I looked down the hill and, in every direction, I looked I saw smoke and flames everywhere.

Everything that was standing was shaken to the ground and was burning.

It was as if the whole world was shaken down and burning.

Stand in awe and watch God's mighty hand in these last days.

I am reminded of a movie 'The Ten Commandments' where Moses stretches out his rod and God parts the Red Sea.

IT WILL BE BIGGER THAN THAT.

A storm is coming, God's storm.

America has a special judgment coming as America has sinned the most and has drug or forced other nations into her abominations.

And in one hour America will be destroyed, maybe not by an earthquake, maybe by war, maybe by an EMP weapon. There are many ways America can be destroyed.

Revelation 18: 4 to 10

And I heard another voice from heaven, saying, Come out of her, my people, that ye be not partakers of her sins, and that ye receive not of her plagues.

[5] For her sins have reached unto heaven, and God hath remembered her iniquities.

[6] Reward her even as she rewarded you, and double unto her double according to her works: in the cup which she hath filled fill to her double.

[7] How much she hath glorified herself, and lived deliciously, so much torment and sorrow give her: for she saith in her heart, I sit a queen, and am no widow, and shall see no sorrow.

[8] Therefore shall her plagues come in one day, death, and mourning, and famine; and she shall be utterly burned with fire: for strong is the Lord God who judgeth her.

[9] And the kings of the earth, who have committed fornication and lived deliciously with her, shall bewail her, and lament for her, when they shall see the smoke of her burning,

[10] Standing afar off for the fear of her torment, saying, Alas, alas that great city Babylon, that mighty city! for in one hour is thy judgment come.

God Bless you and God keep you and yours safe.

As there is no safety anywhere or in anything except in Jesus Christ.

CHAPTER ELEVEN

YOUR TIME HERE DRAWETH NIGH

I am just the dust of the earth, and no one is beneath me, and the only thing special about me is I am forgiven, and I am God's dirt.

Some time ago I had a dream where I was standing on a precipice overlooking a dark gulf before me. But I was not afraid.

A voice from behind me spoke, and as he spoke, he put his hand on my right shoulder and he said:

'YOUR TIME HERE DRAWETH NIGH'.

I woke up confused not knowing if the dream was for me or for all of us?

I prayed and prayed on this dream, (this message).

Since almost all of my contact has been with the Holy Spirit, I felt it was the Holy Spirit speaking to me.

You learn that voice, you know when He speaks to you, you recognize His voice.

As for WHO the message was for; this message was for all of us including me.

Our time here draweth nigh. For Christians, this means you have very little time left to get your loved ones to the safety of Jesus Christ.

You have precious little time left to work in the Lord to bring in lost souls.

In these very last days, you need to carry your Bible everywhere you go. You need to say the blessing over every meal, and you need to repent of sin every time you pray.

The reason being, these are the last days and sin is in everything, even in the food we eat, our drinks, our medications in everything.

Look up HEK 293 and you will see what I am talking about, and today there are even worse things than HEK 293.

You need to say the blessing over every single meal you eat. You need to be apart, separate, a peculiar people unto the Lord.

People need just to look at you and know you are somehow different from other people. You need to be not ashamed to be a Christian but you need to hold up your faith as a flame and not hide it under a bushel basket.

We often eat at a restaurant that serves alcohol (we do NOT drink any alcohol). I always have my Bible with me and I place it on the table in that restaurant and I say the blessing over our food. I will not be ashamed of Jesus, His word or what He has done for me and what He means to me.

You need to talk to friends, neighbors, co-workers, relatives everyone about the saving grace of Jesus Christ and how he loved them so very much that he died for them.

These are the last days, work in the Lord while the sun still shines. Bring in lost souls to the safety of Jesus Christ.

You say you do not want to offend anyone or be a pest.
How offended will your loved ones be in Hell?
And you do not want them pointing a finger at you claiming that YOU never told them just how important Jesus really was. It's time to be a pest, it's time to offend as YOUR time to act is almost UP.

Mark 8: 38

Whosoever therefore shall be ashamed of me and of my words in this adulterous and sinful generation; of him also shall the Son of man be ashamed, when he cometh in the glory of his Father with the holy angels.

God Bless You

God keep you and yours in His loving arms.

CHAPTER TWELVE

TEKEL

How do I make a whole chapter of a book about 'one word'?

If it's from the Holy Spirit, it is a powerful word and being FROM the Holy Spirit it is always in truth.

I do not believe I have ever been given a more powerful one-word message from God.

Every dream I have ever been given has been about America or involved America. And when I was shown world-wide catastrophic events, the focus of my dreams has always been about America.

I know there is much more to the world than America, and I am NOT saying America is special or above any other country. But God has a special judgment laid out for America and that is why my dreams have all involved America.

To whom much is given, much is required.

America has become a cesspool of filth and abomination, and has influenced the whole world to join in her Abominations.

The stench of this sin has reached the nostrils of God – so now God acts.

On Aug. 18th 2018 I was sleeping and the Holy Spirit came to me in a dream. I never saw anyone; I never saw anything. But I know the voice of the Holy Spirit because He has spoken to me on many occasions.

I felt a peace, I felt love, I felt safety and secure being near the Holy Spirit.

The Holy Spirit spoke only 'ONE WORD'.

And that word was (TEKEL).

Then the dream ended.

When I woke up I knew that word was from the book of Daniel.

So, I looked it up.

The full message that was written on the Babylonian palace wall by the very hand of God was.

ME – NE – ME – NE – TE – KEL – U – PHAR – SIN.

When the king of Babylon Belshazzar saw this message being written by the hand of God on his palace walls his knees began to knock in fear.

Daniel 5: 3 to 6

3 Then they brought the golden vessels that were taken out of the temple of the house of God which was at Jerusalem; and the king, and his princes, his wives, and his concubines, drank in them.

4 They drank wine, and praised the gods of gold, and of silver, of brass, of iron, of wood, and of stone.

5 In the same hour came forth fingers of a man's hand, and wrote over against the candlestick upon the plaister of the

wall of the king's palace: and the king saw the part of the hand that wrote.

⁶ Then the king's countenance was changed, and his thoughts troubled him, so that the joints of his loins were loosed, and his knees smote one against another.

This is the interpretation:

ME – NE – God hath numbered the kingdom and finished it.

PE – RES - Thy kingdom is divided and given to the Medes and Persians.

TE – KEL – Thou art weighed in the balances and art found wanting

Remember America IS Babylon.

And America has been weighed and found wanting.

And just like ancient Babylon was destroyed in one night, America also shall be destroyed in one night, in one hour.

I told you the Holy Spirit has been bringing up my old dreams refreshing them, and reminding me of missing details so with that I am prompted to make a new video about many of my old dreams.

And like the king of Babylon, you have been warned.

On that very night the hand writing appeared on the palace walls the Medes and Persians snuck through the walls of Babylon and Babylon the great fell that very night without a fight.

The king of Babylon and all his court were all slain that night.

God is sending signs (warnings) everywhere, in the moon, the sun, stars, in the earth, the seasons, the weather, earthquakes, volcanoes, even our economy, our rulers, our laws, society everywhere you look, you see signs of the soon return of Jesus Christ to Rapture His faithful off this dying world.

Yes God is about to destroy Babylon AGAIN. But this Babylon is America. America will fall and America will never rise again.

I have seen it, I was told this in many ways. Read Jeremiah 50, 51 and Revelation 18 and see that it IS America that God is talking about.

And just like ancient Babylon our days are numbered.

NOW, is the time to humble yourself before Almighty God, repent of sin and beg the blood of Jesus to wash all your sin away, to wash you clean and to make you white as snow.

Then to beg Jesus to enter your heart and lead you and to guide your every step and to give you a new heart.

We are not promised tomorrow.

My prayer and my only goal is to be pleasing to God.

I care NOT, of money in the bank or fancy cars or fancy homes, NOT even jet airplanes.

I see these things as just trapping of the world to pull us away from Jesus Christ.

THE ONLY ONE WHO CAN TRULY SAVE ANYONE FROM WHAT IS SHORTLY TO COME UPON THIS DYING WORLD.

I am just an old, beat up, disabled Vietnam era veteran. Who God touched, who God blessed with dreams and visions and who God asked, to give to you a warning.

I lay NOT my treasure up in this world BUT I lay up my treasure in heaven where moth or rust cannot destroy.

Where do you lay up your treasure?

As we are close, SO VERY CLOSE TO GOING HOME.

There is no safety in anything of this earth, the only way to survive what is soon to come –

IS TO NOT BE HERE – AS IN BEING RAPTURED.

That is our salvation.

That is our safety.

And that is the promise of God.

To save His Remnant off this dying world before the catastrophe hits. Before the Medes and the Persians come crashing through the gates.

God Bless you and God keep you and yours in His loving arms JUST LIKE HE HELD ME.

WITH MUCH LOVE AND MORE GRACE FROM ABOVE

AMEN

CHAPTER THIRTEEN

FEMA Camp dream

I want to tell you about a dream I had gotten from the Holy Spirit.

I dreamed I was in a FEMA camp along with many people. They had armed guards everywhere, and if you got to close to the fence they would shoot to kill.

I dreamed we were worked every day, from sun up until just before sun down. We had different jobs, and if they had nothing for us to do they would have us pick up rocks in the parking lot, just to put them back down again, but this one day they had us working in fields under armed guard of course.

We were not supposed to talk, but we would whisper what we could to each other to communicate. And one day the topic was they had more prisoners coming in and they had to make more room, also they were supposed to be younger prisoners.

We knew what that meant for us, so we worked harder to try to impress the guards that we could do anything that younger people could do.

Toward the end of the day, they marched us back into the camp. They lined us up like normal for evening roll call. When they were satisfied with the count, they marched our entire section out of the camp to a new area I had never seen before.

There they shot us with machine guns, and after they shot us they walked up and down the rows of dead people shooting anyone showing any signs of life.

You may ask, why didn't I get shot? Because I was there in spirit form like a fly on the wall, a witness to the massacre.

I believe that FEMA camps may start out as innocent entities, but will morph into something akin to something much, much worse. And as more prisoners come in they will by necessity have to make room for the new people coming in.

I saw this in my dream, this is what I saw and I cannot take it back or change what I saw.

Matthew 24: 12
And because iniquity shall abound, the love of many shall wax cold.

I pray it will not be so, BUT look where we are headed with our country, need I say more?

This will originally be for the unvaxxed and then the homeless and because the economy collapses everyone will be homeless and they will try to stuff everyone into FEMA camps. That will cause massive overcrowding and the subsequent measures to alleviate the overcrowding.

The Holy Spirit came to me in my dream and told me: 'MUCH MORE PAIN WAS TO COME'.

It should be obvious to everyone that God is lifting his hand of protection from this world and as He does Satan is taking more and more control of this earth.

For many years America has been blessed by God and we had it so good.

But not anymore.

As America has become an abomination in God's eye. And God is about to deal with America very harshly.

The Jews who were God's own chosen people who he freed from captivity in Egypt, parted the Red Sea for them, feed them manna from heaven and gave them drink in the desert. God loved them so very much as they were His chosen people.

Look how harsh God dealt with Israel, after they turned away from God and started worshiping idols. God sent them into bondage in Babylon for 70 years and then God dispersed the Jews all over the world for almost 2000 years and ONLY recently brought them back to their homeland, just as He promised, He would do in the Last Days.

IF God dealt with His chosen people that harsh, WHAT DO WE EXPECT GOD TO DO TO AMERICA?

God will not turn a blind eye toward sin.

The Holy Spirit also gave me this:

BEFORE ONE WOE ENDS ANOTHER WOE BEGINS

This is ONLY the beginning of our troubles. We have only just started into the Time of Sorrows, (Birth Pains if you will) MUCH MORE PAIN IS TO COME.

But if you are in the will and grace of Jesus Christ you have nothing to fear.

Soon, very soon comes the Rapture of the faithful, and then Tribulation (hell) comes to the earth.

As God comes to the wicked as an avenger, he comes to the righteous as a redeemer.

Isaiah the prophet wrote 26:12 "The Lord is going to keep you in perfect peace – if you'll simply trust him".

The Lord says I haven't given you a spirit of fear but of power, love and sound mind. 2 Timothy 1:7.

Even in the most difficult of times we will enjoy great blessing because God will reveal Himself as never before.

As God parted the Red Sea and feed his children Manna from heaven God loves you just that much also.

Acts 2:17 And it shall come to pass in the last days saith God, I will pour out my spirit upon all flesh.

We are all truly blessed to be alive at this time in history, to be a witness to God's heavy hand upon the whole earth, but especially America.

Because we who are faithful and, in the will, and grace of Jesus Christ will be called home very soon. In the twinkling of an eye, we will be Raptured out of here and we will go home and we will leave this vile and sin filled world behind.

And where we go there will not even be a word for sin.

I know because I was Raptured twice.

BUT I never made it to heaven in my first Rapture dream, (you see I woke up right when I started going up). But in that dream Jesus came down to me in a beam of light and He held me in His loving arms and I looked into the eyes of God.

He never spoke a word but His eyes said: 'WELCOME HOME I LOVE YOU AND I HAVE MISSED YOU SO VERY MUCH'.

But right when we started to go up, I woke up.

My second Rapture dream, I made it to heaven, but I opened my eyes and I was in this huge reception hall that was full of people. Everyone there was young, trim, fit, and wearing brilliant white robe with a sash around their middle and wearing sandals on their feet. And right when we started to go outside to see Jesus I woke up.

I was told I still had a work to do for the Lord, here on the earth.

Now I will spend the rest of my life trying to get back to that place where I was before, BACK IN THE ARMS OF JESUS.

What I saw was LOVE, a love beyond understanding, beyond words.

So much LOVE that He was willing to shed His blood for you and for me, to be beaten and tortured for us, He was even nailed to an old rugged cross for us and HE DIED FOR YOU AND FOR ME.

NO GREATER LOVE HAS ANY MAN FOR HIS FRIENDS THAN HE LAY DOWN HIS LIFE FOR HIM.

Jesus loves you and me that much.

There is no other name in heaven or on earth that can save you from what is shortly to come upon this earth.

Are you betting these things will NOT happen?

Look back one year remember how things were, you never imagined that things would get as bad as they are now.

BECAUSE TODAY WAS JUST LIKE YESTERDAY DOES NOT MEAN THAT TOMORROW WILL BE LIKE TODAY!

BE PREPARED as Jesus is coming back, just like He said.

ARE YOU PREPARED FOR THAT? The Rapture.

Humble yourself, repent of all your sin, forgive your enemy's, and pray and invite Jesus Christ into your heart as your Lord and Savior. And believe that Jesus Christ is the Son of God.

Read your King James Bible, associate with likeminded believers (and NOT these false teachers). Who are only interested in your money and not your soul.

DO NOT FOLLOW A CHURCH, A FAITH, A RELIGION, A PREACHER, A TEACHER OR EVEN A MAN, DO NOT EVEN FOLLOW ME - BUT FOLLOW JESUS CHRIST AND HIS WORD ONLY IN THE KING JAMES BIBLE.

Yes by all means try to find a church of likeminded believers who worship God and His only begotten Son Jesus Christ, who teach & preach the full Bible, repentance, Hell, Revelation ALL OF THE BIBLE.

As Jesus is the Way, the Truth and the Life.

In these very last days, hours and minutes REMEMBER that what we say and what we do is more important than you could ever imagine.

We keep you and yours in our prayers

CHAPTER FOURTEEN
Judgment comes, the Big BOOM

I am only a tool like a saw, or a hammer hanging, in the Master Carpenters tool shed for Him to use.

My only reason and purpose for being here, is to work, glorify, worship, honor and obey, and to be pleasing to the Master Carpenter (Jesus Christ).

I was emailing a good friend and Brother in Christ Gary up in Ohio, and then my conversation turned and it was the Holy Spirit that took over my writing and started giving me the words to type, and this is what I told him:

I am praying to be found worthy to escape what is to come soon upon the entire world.

But especially America, because America has sinned the most and drug or forced other countries into her abominations.

America has a separate judgment and is set aside from the judgment that is to come upon the entire world.

America will be judged very harshly.
She will fall and never rise again.
Where no man will be found in her anymore.
No light will shine in her anymore.
No singing and no music will be heard in her anymore at all.
America will become desolate and barren from the Pacific to the Atlantic.
Like scorched earth.
God has proclaimed it, AS IT IS WRITTEN, SO SHALL IT BE DONE.

And only the hissing of serpents will be heard in her anymore.

Then later I was given this:
To whom much is given, MUCH IS EXPECTED.

God's judgment comes.

NOW PRAYING FOR AMERICA IS LIKE PRAYING FOR A DEAD MAN!

NOW IT'S LIKE WATCHING THE CLOCK TICK DOWN TO AN EXECUTION.

And IF it were NOT for the blood of Jesus, WE ALL WOULD HAVE A DATE WITH THE EXECUTIONER.

Then the very night that happened I had a rather unusual dream. I was lying in bed TRYING to get to sleep, BUT sleep would NOT come it was about 3 AM.

THEN ALL OF A SUDDEN, my whole house started shaking, my room was shaking, my bed was shaking and even my bedroom window started rattling.

The shaking lasted only about 10 to 15 seconds and then I heard the loudest BOOOOM I have ever heard.

It was what you imagine an atomic bomb sounding like off in the distance.

I cried out: DID YOU HEAR THAT

Was I awake - or was I dreaming.

I didn't know.

IF I was dreaming, then I was dreaming I was IN MY BED trying to sleep.

And all that happened as part of my dream.

HAVE YOU EVER HEARD OF SUCH A THING???

The next morning, I jumped up and checked all the local and state news outlets to see IF they mentioned any explosion, earthquake or an asteroid strike or anything major like that.

BUT NOTHING.

CAN YOU EXPLAIN IT TO ME???

Have you ever had a dream that was so real, that was about you lying in bed and you were actually in bed? And then something happens and you dream you react to it, I see this as a warning that something is coming and soon.

YOU HAVE BEEN WARNED.

Now is the time to repent of sin, to humble yourself before Almighty God and beg forgiveness of you sin. To plead the blood of Jesus wash over you and wash all your sin away, to wash you clean of sin, to wash you as white as snow.

And beg Jesus come into your heart and give you a new heart that you be born again and for Jesus to lead you and to guide your steps all the days of your life.

The executioner comes.

Our time here is very, VERY short.

Soon we the faithful in Jesus Christ WE will be called home.

We will be Raptured OFF this dying world.

We will leave this world to Satan and Satan will rule with an iron fist and Satan's wrath will be poured out without mercy and without measure, also God's wrath will be poured out in like manor and the people will be in the middle.

And this is why Billions will die in the Tribulation.

Can you NOT see this? Can you NOT see this is happening and THIS is where all this is headed, right now in a slow progressive way, a little more every day.

But just like Birth Pains this is speeding up, faster and faster and stronger and stronger.

Have you noticed TIME seems to have sped up? NOW even TIME SEEMS TO BE MOVING FASTER AND FASTER.

IT'S COMING

Tribulation is bearing down on us, BUT first comes the Rapture of the faithful.

1 Corinthians 2:9
But as it is written, Eye hath not seen, nor ear heard, neither have entered into the heart of man, the things which God hath prepared for them that love him.

I told you heaven would be beyond words. I have revealed many things about heaven. BUT there is much more that has NOT been revealed than what was revealed. There are many secrets about heaven that are kept from us. Of those things you must have faith in God.

I told you the saints in heaven will have power:

1 Corinthians 6:3 Know ye not that we shall judge angels? How much more things that pertain to this life?

We have the promise of God to rescue us off this dying world.

1 Thessalonians 5:9 For God hath NOT appointed us to wrath, but to obtain salvation by our Lord Jesus Christ.

YOU are a precious child of the Most High Living God, who loves you and who treasures YOU above all the gold of the earth and above all the stars of heaven.

And we and I love and treasure you as well.

We keep YOU and yours in our prayers.

BUT we especially pray for the lost as they have NO IDEA of what is coming RIGHT AT THEM.

HELL ON EARTH - IS WHAT IS COMING.

The ONLY way to escape what is coming upon this dying world - IS TO NOT BE HERE.

As in being Raptured.

Pray, read your Bible, repent of sin, and be in the will of Almighty God.

Pray to be found worthy to escape what is coming.

God Bless you and God keep you and yours in His loving arms, JUST LIKE HE HELD ME.

WITH MUCH LOVE AND MORE GRACE FROM ABOVE

AMEN

CHAPTER FIFTEEN

Get Thee Into Darkness

I weep for the lost because they have no earthly idea of just what is coming straight at them.

I know because I have seen it, and that is why I weep.

Too much horror to even imagine.

I know many of my dreams involves pain, suffering, death and destruction BUT my message is one of HOPE, GRACE and LOVE and to remind people there is salvation from what is to come upon the earth. There is ONE and ONLY ONE who can save you, me or anyone from what is to come upon this dying world. And that one is Jesus Christ.

God made many promises to us, His faithful, and I am placing ALL my faith and trust on Jesus Christ the Son of God and the WORD of God, because there is NOTHING else you can place your faith in.

I had a dream.

I dreamed I was high up above the earth in the spirit and a stillness and a quiet covered all the land. Looking down upon America all I saw was darkness and it covered the whole land.

Normally America from very high up is covered in lights and it looks like a shinning jewel from space. But not this time.

I came down near the earth and I saw every home was black and I saw families sleeping on mattresses out in the yard or on the front porch because it was just too hot to sleep in their homes.

And the heat was unbearable and there was NO relief.

As there was no power, so nothing worked, and all of America was quiet and in darkness.

Vehicles would not start or run, nothing electronic would work. Nothing worked, no cell phones, no TV, no radio, no lights, no heat, no air conditioning, nothing at all seemed to work.

It even seemed batteries and all electronics were dead.

Everything was dead and NOW the people remaining, were dying also.

There was a very eerie silence that covered all of America a deathly silence as that was what it was death.

And people all over America were sleeping outdoors, and they were dying.

They died from lack of water, lack of food, exposure, heat stroke, bad water, as many were drinking water out of creeks, streams, swimming pools anywhere they could find water, because they were that thirsty.

And there was a plague upon the land a pestilence and that was killing people as well. Death was everywhere in America the smell of death permeated everywhere and everything.

It seemed that every yard, every parking lot had dead bodies decaying in it.

But there was ONE thing that I remember the MOST and that was the silence. As there was stone silence over all the land. I heard no birds chirping, no crickets or frogs NOTHING but STONE SILENCE.

You could not hear any airplanes, trains, cars, no music, no one talked, no one said a thing. And it seemed if they did talk, they whispered so quiet as if they were afraid someone would hear them.

The people knew that the wrath of God had come down upon them.

I saw home after home and they were ALL dark and in total silence.

And everyone was sleeping outdoors in the dark.

It seemed as if the people were beat and they knew it.

They just gave up and sat in silent bewilderment waiting to die.

And death would come quickly to most of them.

This is what I saw.

I'll tell you what God gives me.

I could sugar coat things and tell you America will come back bigger and stronger than before.

BUT I was commanded to tell you the truth just as it was given to me.

A couple years ago the Holy Spirit told me this: NOW PRAYING FOR AMERICA WAS LIKE PRAYING FOR A DEAD MAN.

And you know why we do not pray for the dead.

I was given scripture with this dream. I can always tell when God wants to confirm a dream and by doing so, He stresses the importance of the dream as well.

I was given.

Isaiah 47:5

Sit thou silent, and get thee into darkness, O daughter of the Chaldeans: for thou shall no more be called The Lady of Kingdoms.

The Lady of Kingdoms is America.

Our time here is very short.

Now what we say and do is more important than ever as these are the Last Days.

And we are in the Time of Sorrows or (the Birth Pains) and just like birth pains our pain and suffering will increase with frequency and severity as time draws to a close for the believer.

NOW is the time to repent of sin, humble yourself, get in the will and grace of Jesus Christ.

To be pleasing to God, IS EVERYTHING.

It is time to come out of the world and to stand with Jesus Christ who loves you so very much, much more than you could ever know.

Now is NOT the time to deny Jesus in any way and to repent of sin every time you pray, to carry your Bible everywhere you can and to say the blessing over every meal you eat.

NOW is NOT the TIME TO DENY JESUS.

Because IF you do so, then Jesus will deny you to the Father.

Mark 8:38
Whosoever therefore shall be ashamed of me and of my words in this adulterous and sinful generation: of him also shall the Son of Man be ashamed, when he cometh in the glory of his Father with the holy angels.

These are the very LAST DAYS spoke of by Jesus in Matthew and WE ARE THAT LAST GENERATION.

We pray for all of you.

But we especially pray for the lost because they have no idea of just what is coming straight at them.

WITH MUCH LOVE AND MORE GRACE FROM ABOVE

AMEN

CHAPTER SIXTEEN

Standing At The Judgment Table

In 2016 we were having a real problem in paying our tithes, and donating to our church and we struggled with our bills and with what we were supposed to give to our church. We knew this was God's money and we knew we were supposed to pay God first and everything else second. As God does not like being second or third on your list.

Then I had a dream and, in this dream, I was standing at a long table with a white tablecloth on it. Now this table went out of my sight to my right and out of sight to my left.

I remember feeling like there were a lot of people behind me waiting their turn but I never turned to look at them. I never heard a word from them, but I just felt their presence behind me patiently waiting their turn.

I was thinking that it was such a waste of space, to have such a long white table in this huge room. There was a chair and I went up and I sat in the chair and across from me sat a bearded man in sandals, kind of long brown hair and a long white robe. I remember, I was ashamed, and I refused to look up into the eyes of this man.

The man never introduced himself, I felt he needed no introduction, I knew who he was. I was ashamed, as I knew I had not done right in my tithes to God. I was also scared as to what would happen to me.

There was a huge book on the table in front of the man, and he opened the book and started to read. I never said a word, and he didn't ask any questions and it seemed He already knew who I was.

As he read it he would make little sounds like um, uh hu, mmmm and he would turn a page and do the same over and over until he came to one page where he stopped.

The man stared at the page and didn't say a word for a long while, finally he spoke up and said: **'I have never seen this before, you're our first one'** and then he paused.

Still not looking up, I sheepishly asked: 'What'?

The man with the beard and the long robe scratched his beard and said: **'Congratulations, You're our Million Dollar Winner'**.

I was floored, my mouth literally dropped open, but still I would not look up into the eyes of this man, I was still ashamed and afraid.

Then the man in the Robe asked: 'What part of that is yours, and what part of that is God's part?'

Then numbers escaped me and I had no concept of numbers and I could not think but I tried to answer and I said: 'I don't know Lord, is it $10,000, is it $100,000, I don't know, you tell me?'

I found myself negotiating with the man in the white robe.

Then I woke up, and I went to the foot of my bed, and I got on my knees, and I cried and I prayed.

I told the Lord it's all yours I want no part of this, it's all yours and to please forgive me…

A short time after this dream I went to Michigan for a short vacation.
While I was there, I went to my old General Motors Union Hall to check to see if I had any retirement coming since I had worked for General Motors for over 11 years.

The nice lady there told me I had $188.00 coming from my retirement account every month from General Motors.

I was thinking that since General Motors filed bankruptcy, I didn't think I had anything coming at all.

Then I remembered my dream and how it was all the Lord's money.

I give that money as my tithes, my Kindle money from the sales from my books goes to support this Last Days ministry mailing out Bibles, books, CDs.

That money is about $40 to $60 per month. (But it's all God's money).

Then I realized the Lord made a way for me to pay my tithes from money I didn't even know I had coming.

Our church that we first started attending changed pastors, as our paster retired and the new pastor banned me from speaking.

So, we went in search of a new church.

Thank You Jesus. God always makes a way for us!

God is always surprising and never fails to surprise us and inspire us every day.

Always make God first in everything and God will reward you for it.

Like the time I sent $75.00 to a Jewish relief fund in Israel and within 7 days I got a surprise and totally unexpected refund for overpayment on our escrow account for $749.00

Tell me God is not awesome.

Or the time I needed a new computer and the parts list came to $330.00 and someone somewhere sent me $333.00 for a donation to the ministry.

Or the time I needed $1,200.00 for a pallet load of plastic pails to build water filters with. I said only a short prayer and the very next day two Jewish ladies from Israel sent me (you guessed it) $1,200.00 via Western Union.

God has blessed me more than I could ever describe and God will bless you, IF you make God first and never second.

We learn by baby steps to walk by faith and not by sight.

Always put God first and God will put you first.

CHAPTER SEVENTEEN

Strong Delusion

2 Thessalonians 2: 11
And for this cause God shall send them strong delusion, that they should believe a lie

A STRONG DELUSION is coming soon and the whole world will be enthralled and talking about this. Every people and every tongue will be talking about this delusion (this lie) that is to come. All the news for weeks & weeks will be talking about this.

This will be such a strong delusion (lie) that many Christians will be led astray and believe the lie.

It's difficult to describe something you have no frame of reference for, much like a man 2000 years ago describing a modern jumbo jet flying low overhead.

But I will try.

The Holy Spirit told me a strong delusion is coming and the whole world will be taken in by this lie.

BUT I was NOT told specifically what this delusion would be, but I was pointed in a direction.

I thought that it might be Artificial Intelligence, Cloned human beings, hybrids, Transhuman (a mixture of human and machine) or even Chimera's (with a mixture of human and animal DNA).

But when these topics came up I got no response from the Holy Spirit, but when aliens, UFO's, or inter-dimensional beings came up the Holy Spirit in my heart and in my head nudged me as if to say, (this is important), Pay attention.

When you watch the History Channel's 'Ancient Aliens' program you are immediately struck with the fact they have an agenda and they are fast and hard at work promoting 'their' agenda.

That agenda is that aliens have visited us in the far ancient past and right up until today. Also, these ancient aliens 'seeded life' on this planet. So, their logic is we owe them.

They are our progenitors and 'they' are here to save us, ('we are THERE progeny so-to-speak'). And there is a whole slew of books and videos that also promote this false narrative.

They now have many followers who actually believe we are descendants from extraterrestrial beings. And in some cases, this has become a new religion. I believe this is the strong delusion to come.

What is ironic about this topic is that several world-renowned scientists who have researched the alien (UFO) phenomena such as J. Allen Hynek, Jacques Vallee and many others have come to a conclusion. And that conclusion is, that: These are NOT aliens from another world, like Orion's Belt (or some such place) BUT are in fact inter-dimensional beings.

In other words, these alien beings are NOT from another planet in the cosmos but are in fact from planet earth (they are from a different dimension). (Now this fact they do have correct, THEY ARE from a different dimension alright, they are from Hell).

You now have military pilots on the news commenting on gun sight footage of alien craft that their weapons have locked onto. First of all, military personnel sign a non-disclosure agreement and for them to even talk about such classified material publicly would put them in Leavenworth for many years.

Also, the video footage they show is the classified property of the US Government, so just how do they end up with this footage on the news? This (in my opinion) is already soft confirmation; they are preparing us for a major announcement one day soon.

I am led to the fact that this is the great delusion to come. They will release the shocking news that NASA has discovered life on Mars soon. That will soften the news later that we are not alone in the Universe.

So, you will already know and believe in life (that is not of this earth). So, then the next logical step is to announce that Aliens are real and have been visiting earth for thousands of years.

Then will come the NEWS that these same aliens seeded life on the earth. And 'they' have come back to help us with things like curing cancer, growing more food for people, extending human life, curing diseases, creating abundant clean energy and many more wonderful things for the benefit of mankind.

Sounds great, don't it? BUT it's a lie.
They may very well help with some of our problems, but it will have a catch. There is always a price to pay nothing is EVER FREE, not when you are dealing with Satan.

The price will be that every human on the planet must take a DNA upgrade to become like them, to 'evolve' to the next level of evolution. To become more like them. Along with this mark or DNA upgrade you will also have to receive either an RFID implant or receive a Circuit board tattoo either on your right hand or on your forehead. When you receive your RFID or circuit board tattoo you will be marked so everyone can see that you have the MARK.

With this mark you will also receive your DNA upgrade.
ONLY with this mark will you be able to buy, sell, rent, drive a car, get any benefits, retirement, disability, medical, banking everything will be tied to this mark and without it you will eventually be hunted down and eliminated.

There are many benefits to this DNA upgrade, you will live to 400 maybe 500 years old, you will be smarter, trim, run faster, you will look and feel younger, be stronger, be resistant to most all disease, you will heal faster. You will become a super human with this DNA upgrade.

The only problem is that by taking this DNA upgrade it will change your DNA and that change will make you unredeemable to God, as then you will NOT be in God's image but in the image of man (or more correctly Satan).

Revelation 9:6 And in those days shall men seek death, and shall not find it; and shall desire to die, and death shall flee from them. - This is how this scripture is fulfilled.

This was why God destroyed the earth with the flood in the days of Noah. And God is about to destroy the earth again and for the same reason. And as only Noah and his family were perfect in their seed (in their generations, there DNA) and that was why they were saved from the Great flood. That is why God will save us who are faithful and true to him in these last days.

1 Thessalonians 5:9 For God hath not appointed us to wrath, but to obtain salvation by our Lord Jesus Christ.

Remember I am not a profit, I never claimed to be a prophet. I am only a Watchman who receives dreams, visions and contact from the Holy Spirit.

So, if your intent is to criticize you have a lot of ammunition here. But if you have seen my other videos and you know about my dreams and visions, my contact with the Holy Spirit. You have the faith of a mustard seed to at least hear and heed this as a warning and nothing more, then I have succeeded in my goal. Remember, as a Watchman my job is to warn.

You have been warned.

1 Corinthians 13:9 For we know in part and we prophesy in part.

1 Corinthians 13:12 For now we see through a glass darkly.

This scenario fits with all my dreams and visions, what I was shown and what I was told and this scenario is scriptural.

Also keep in mind, there are no prerequisites or preconditions for the Rapture and it will come when you least expect it. So be watching and in prayer for that great Catching Away of the faithful. (Oh Glorious Day)!

As God comes to the wicked as an avenger, he comes to the righteous as a redeemer.

Isaiah the prophet wrote in,
Isaiah 26:12 The Lord is going to keep you in perfect peace – if you'll simply trust him.

The Lord says; I haven't given you a spirit of fear but of power, love and sound mind. 2 Timothy 1:7.

Bad times are coming, but even in the most difficult of times we will enjoy great blessing because God will reveal himself to us and protect us as never before.

Remember - This is all part of God's plan AND GOD IS IN CONTROL.

What I do, I do by, for and through Jesus Christ, as he is the only one who can save you, me or anyone from what is to come upon the earth. When I lower myself, I uplift Jesus.

And Jesus is the only one I must impress that I must please.

If you're not saved RIGHT NOW is the best time to get to know the saving grace of Jesus. Humble yourself before Almighty God and repent of your sins and plead the blood of Jesus wash you white as snow and pray.

Confess with your mouth that you are a sinner in need of salvation from Jesus Christ your Lord and Savior who died on the cross for your sins and mine. But who arose on the 3rd day and who ascended up to Heaven and now sits on the right hand of the Father waiting his Glorious and Triumphant return.

And believe that Jesus is the Son of God.

Be in prayer and watching for that blessed hope, the great catching away of the faithful. As God is about to take us home.

God Bless you and God keep you and yours is my prayer

CHAPTER EIGHTEEN

Three Visions From The Holy Spirit

Do you know why Jeremiah was called the weeping prophet?

He wept over what was lost?

I also weep over what was lost.

The Holy Spirit came to me one night about 8 years ago. I was lying in bed and I was praying with my arms outstretched to heaven and I began shaking in the spirit. And I felt the Holy Spirit all over me like a warm electric blanket. My whole body was shaking in the spirit.

When I settled down and I lowered my hands, the Holy Spirit came to me and He hovered above me I do not think this was a dream, as I was fully awake but I never opened my eyes.

I felt, I sensed the presence of the Holy Spirit hovering above me so close, I could feel His breath upon me. I felt that I could just reach up and touch Him. The Holy Spirit was there above me and he spoke to me in words that I heard with my own ears.

What he said was: **(AMERICA IS ENTERING JUDGMENT)**

I cried and I prayed because I knew what that meant.

(I was reminded to read Jeremiah 50, 51 and Revelation 18).

………………..

Also keep in mind that for many years ocean going ships entering New York City harbor the very first thing they saw or read in the new world is what is on a water tower, it is the name of a city and that city is named BABYLON.

So, ocean going ships leaving America, the last thing they saw OF America is the water tower that proclaims: BABYLON. (Keep that in mind when you read Revelation 18).

God is always surprising and amazing in every way.

……………………………

The Holy Spirit came to me a couple years later and just like before, I could not tell you if I was dreaming or having a vision. I was just lying in bed with my eyes closed. And again, the Holy Spirit hovered above me and spoke to me in words that I heard with my own ears. And like before I never opened my eyes.

And what he said was:
AMERICA IS IN THE TIME OF SORROWS (THE BIRTH PANGS HAVE BEGUN).

I wept and I prayed because I knew what was to come.

Then Holy Spirit came to me a third time a couple of years after that and just like before, I could not tell you if I was dreaming or having a vision. I was just lying in bed with my eyes closed. And again, the Holy Spirit hovered above me and spoke to me in words that I heard with my own ears. And like before I never opened my eyes.

And what he said was:

(PRAYING FOR AMERICA NOW IS LIKE PRAYING FOR A DEAD MAN.) - (AMERICA IS BABYLON AND AMERICA WILL BE DESTROYED IN ONE HOUR)

Again, I was told to read: Jeremiah 50 & 51 and Revelation 18

Again, I wept and I prayed.

Revelation 18:10
Standing afar off for the fear of her torment, saying, Alas, alas that great city Babylon, that mighty city! for in one hour is thy judgment come.

Revelation 18:17
For in one hour so great riches is come to nought. And every shipmaster, and all the company in ships, and sailors, and as many as trade by sea, stood afar off.

Revelation 18:19
And they cast dust on their heads, and cried, weeping and wailing, saying, Alas, alas that great city, wherein were made rich all that had ships in the sea by reason of her costliness! for in one hour is she made desolate.

Revelation 18:21
And a mighty angel took up a stone like a great millstone, and cast it into the sea, saying, Thus with violence shall that great city Babylon be thrown down, and shall be found no more at all.

Revelation 18:22
And the voice of the harpers, and musicians, and the pipers, and the trumpeters, shall be heard no more at all in thee; and no craftsman, of whatsoever craft he be, shall be found any more in thee; and the sound of a millstone shall be heard no more at all in thee.

Revelation 18: 23
And the light of a candle shall shine no more at all in thee; and the voice of the bridegroom and of the bride shall be heard no more at all in thee: for thy merchants were the great nen of the earth; for by thy sorceries were all nations deceived.

I am not the only one seeing this and saying this, you have Pastor David Wilkerson, Henry Gruver, Dumitru Duduman and many, many others who have had their own dreams and visions regarding the destruction of America by God. A coming cataclysmic judgment that IS coming to America that God showed them.

God told them to warn as to what is coming, much like God told me to WARN of destruction, judgment to come.

Now 20 years ago this may have seemed far off in the distant future, BUT NOW YOU CAN SEE IT ALL COMING TOGETHER AND JUDGMENT COMES.

I was TOLD to: **'WAKE UP AND TELL THE PEOPLE'.**

And that is what I have been trying to do ever since.

1 Thessalonians 5: 3
For when they shall say, Peace and safety; then sudden destruction cometh upon them, as travail upon a woman with child; and they shall not escape.

1 Thessalonians 5: 9
For God hath not appointed us to wrath, but to obtain salvation by our Lord Jesus Christ,

2 Timothy 1:7
For God hath not given us the spirit of fear; but of power, and of love, and of a sound mind.

The Rapture is soon, are you ready?

NOW is the time to get ready as you do not want to wake up and find yourself in the Tribulation.

Jesus is the only one who can save you, me or anyone from what is to come shortly upon this earth.

Remember above all things: GOD IS IN CONTROL

CHAPTER NINTEEN
My Movie Theater Dream

WE are Standing on the precipice of an abyss with no bottom.

EVERYTHING collapses (I mean EVERYTHING)

And Jesus is our only salvation.

In the Fall of 2017, I had a dream and, in that dream, where I walked into a very large and plush movie theater it had curtains on the walls from the ceiling to the floor. There was a huge curtain covering the screen. I walked down to the front row and sat down in the center. The curtains and the seats were all a gold color. The seats were very plush and comfortable.

I was sitting all alone in this huge plush theater on the front row which I thought was odd because I never sit in the front row. I remember looking behind me looking to see if there was anyone else in this huge theater, but I was all alone.

When all of a sudden, the lights went down slowly and the curtains were pulled back very slowly revealing a huge, very white and shiny screen. Then the movie started to play, but there was no introduction, no name, no credits or anything, the movie just started to play. I thought that was very strange.

The movie I estimated to be about 5 minutes but honestly it could have been 10 minutes or longer (it is impossible to guess time in a dream.)

What I saw, what I was shown was a whole shopping list of different ways America was to be destroyed. One right after another without stopping or pausing. And the movie just kept on playing without comment or explanation.

I saw nuclear weapons going off in most major American cities. I saw foreign troops on American soil. I saw what I thought was an asteroid strike hit the earth in what looked like western Canada.

What I saw was a massive rock going into the ocean and I reasoned it to be an asteroid. But now I think about it and it could have been the volcanic mountain at

La Palma going into the ocean, I do not really know. What I was shone was a massive rock hitting the ocean causing a monster of a Tsunami. Causing a massive wall of water to hit America's East coast. And all the coasts of the Atlantic Ocean.

Revelation 8: 8 to 11
And the second angel sounded, and as it were a great mountain burning with fire was cast into the sea: and the third part of the sea became blood;

9 And the third part of the creatures which were in the sea, and had life, died; and the third part of the ships were destroyed.

10 And the third angel sounded, and there fell a great star from heaven, burning as it were a lamp, and it fell upon the third part of the rivers, and upon the fountains of waters;

11 And the name of the star is called Wormwood: and the third part of the waters became wormwood; and many men died of the waters, because they were made bitter.

Many times, I am shown things but I am not given an explanation for what I was shown. In that case I must pray the Holy Spirit give me an explanation of what I was shown or points me to scripture explaining in more detail of what I was given.

And then you have this detail that not all things are to be revealed. So, I might be given an odd dream and the Holy Spirit will confirm that it was a prophetic dream but then I get no explanation of what I was shown. Such is the case with Revelation 8: 8 I am not shown or told IF this is an asteroid or La Palma sliding into the Atlantic Ocean.

And what does it matter, as a tsunami is still a tsunami no matter how it is generated it is STILL coming.

I saw A mega-earthquake on the west coast that caused two other faults to rip wide open causing another massive Tsunami on the West Coast. Then these earthquakes caused several major Volcanoes to erupt. I saw the New Madrid fault rupture which ripped America in half from the Great Lakes down to New Orleans and this was up to a hundred of miles wide at some points.

America's heartland was turned into a great sea between two continents. And I saw Yellowstone erupt with a massive eruption. I saw several other volcanos all erupting at the same time. I was above the earth witnessing all this. But then I zoomed down and in close and I saw civil war in America. I saw Americans shooting and bombing other American's. Everyone seemed to have gone mad, rioting, looting, burning and much murder in the streets. I saw paper money blowing down the street and no one gave it a thought as it was worthless paper.

Ezekiel 7:19
They shall cast their silver in the streets, and their gold shall be removed: their silver and their gold shall not be able to deliver them in the dayof the wrath of the Lord: they shall not satisfy their souls, neither fill their bowels: because it is the stumblingblock of their iniquity.

I saw America in darkness from coast to coast it was in total darkness. I saw what looked like a super bright flash high up in space over America and then the lights just rolled out across America. America turns dark and cold and the lights went out all over America as if an EMP weapon had been used against America.

When you see photos today of America from space at night, America looks like a brilliant jewel all shinning as there are lights everywhere. But I saw America go dark and quiet. I only saw this for a moment but my impression was that it was from some kind of attack upon America.

Isaiah 47:5
Sit thou silent, and get thee into darkness, O daughter of the Chaldeans: for thou shalt no more be called, The lady of kingdoms.

Everyone was starving and people were eating bugs, bark, leaves and grass as the hunger was so great. I saw people cooking and eating other people. I saw parents cooking and eating their children. I saw parents trading their children for a hand full of rice or beans. Cannibalism was so rampant that no one gave it a thought as it had become common and normal.

What I saw was in the Great Tribulation and I have had several dreams about that period of time. And my impression was, this is NOT off in our distant future but was our near present time. I saw much, much more! My focus was America as America has sinned the most and drug or forced other nations into her abominations. But no part of the earth was spared, every nation, every island, every people, everywhere was touched by this Great Tribulation.

I saw nuclear weapons detonated over America's major cities, Riots and Civil War, Hurricane's hitting America, Asteroid Strikes, Tsunamis on the East Coast and Tsunamis on the West Coast, Earthquakes, Volcanoes erupting. The sun started to burn up crops, trees and finally it scorched and kill many people.

I saw war coming to America. I zoomed in and I saw what looked like economic collapse where the dollar will be worthless, as it was blowing in the wind down the streets and no one cared. Money was worthless, gold was worthless the only thing that had real value was FOOD & CLEAN WATER.

I saw people bartering items to trade, as they didn't want dollars, they didn't even want silver or gold. But, everyone wanted food, everyone was hungry. And there was very little food and what food there was, was unaffordable at any price.

People were eating cats, dogs, rats then grass, leaves, bark anything to alleviate those terrible gnawing hunger pains that never stopped day or night. People would literally trade their children for a handful of beans or rice and I saw that also.

Pestilence and disease were rampant and killed many.

Exposure, bad food, bad water killed many.

Many died for not getting medications they needed to stay alive.

There was no food, no water, no medications of any kind, men went mad, billions of demons were released upon the earth and they entered many people making them do unspeakable things.

Ask yourself why the fallen angels fell from heaven?

They mated with human women who bore them great children giants (or Nephilim). Fallen angels, demons, Nephilim will all walk the earth in the Tribulation and their destruction of mankind will be very great. The Bible says in

Revelation 9:14 & 15 that four fallen angels will be released and they will kill 1/3 of mankind on the earth in the Last Days. I saw that as well.

Diseases run rampant; people lived like filthy animals scurrying underground for protection. I saw people eating people, as there was no food. I was shown that this was the fate of those left behind after the Rapture.

When I woke up from this dream I was gasping for air and crying at this terrible scene I was just shown. I immediately got on my knees at the foot of my bed and I cried and I prayed…

I was shown many horrific things in the Tribulation. From what I was shown I absolutely DO NOT WANT TO ENTER THE TRIBULATION.

Bad things are coming upon this earth.

And the ONLY way to survive what is to come upon this dying world – IS TO NOT BE HERE!

As in being Raptured.

And the ONLY way to get Raptured is to repent of your sin, beg the blood of Jesus to cover you, wash you clean and wash all your sin away. And to beg Jesus to enter your heart as your Lord and savior.

Do you see why it is so critically important NOW to get saved and, in the will, and grace of Jesus Christ?

Believe me you do not want to get left behind as what is coming will be nothing short of Hell On Earth.

On the news right now, they are talking about shortages, price increases, limits on purchases. Many grocery stores have OVERNIGHT doubled their prices on all their food items. Can you NOT see where this is headed?

The government and top economist are warning of an economic collapse even greater than the 1929 crash is coming and soon.

And now our banks have started to collapse, this will continue. Major banks in Europe will collapse and drag the whole world into an economic abyss.

Very soon, EVERYTHING COLLAPSES.

In my dream I saw a multitude of ways America would be destroyed. They are ALL coming and soon.

It has already started.

So, the rapture MUST be very close, any day now.

Signs are everywhere and, in your face, - BUT the biggest sign is the convergence of ALL these signs together at the same time.

The Bible says when you see all these things LOOK UP for your redemption draweth nigh.

So, very, VERY soon we are going home, to be with our Jesus in the clouds.

We will walk on streets of pure gold, the thing of such value here on this earth we will walk on it in heaven.

NOW, TODAY is the time to get right with God as tomorrow is NOT promised.

Consider what I saw, even if only just several of these things come true you still would NOT want to endure what is coming.

I BEG YOU, These ARE the Very Last Days and we are in the last minutes and Last seconds. Please get right with God.

Because what is coming will be NOTHING compared to torment in hell for eternity.

I am sorry if my words offended anyone BUT the hour is late and I must do what I must, to let people realize what is coming right at them.

I was commanded to: WAKE UP AND TELL THE PEOPLE.

And to that end I have done all that I have done.

Not for me, not for my glory, not to make money. I do NOT care about money as from my perspective it will all become worthless one day soon anyway. SO, what you can do WITH your money today is more important than what you will be able to do with it later.

I do all that I do to honor and glorify my God and savior Jesus Christ and HIM ONLY.

As I am only the dust of the earth. BUT I AM GOD'S DIRT.

God Bless you and God keep you and yours safe.

WITH MUCH LOVE AND MORE GRACE FROM ABOVE

AMEN

CHAPTER TWENTY

My Two Tsunami Dreams

Jeremiah 51:42 The sea is come up upon Babylon; she is covered with the multitude of the waves thereof.

Jeremiah 51: 55 Because the Lord hath spoiled Babylon, and destroyed out of her the great voice; when her waves do roar like great waters, a noise of their voice is uttered.

So many people have had Tsunami dreams, SO VERY MANY.

There are thousands maybe millions of people who have had Tsunami dreams.

I had two Tsunami dreams that were coming upon America.

I saw the east coast and the west coast inundated with much water.
And millions died, millions were homeless, destruction was everywhere.

The west coast Tsunami was caused by an earthquake (I think in the Cascadia area). The rupture went from northern California all the way to Canada. I heard people talking and they were saying it was a 9.4.   And the earthquake caused very much destruction all along the north west coast, Seattle, Tacoma, Portland and all the cities along the north west coast were destroyed by the earthquake.

But then came the Tsunami in short order and washed everything away many miles inland. Everything was destroyed either by the very violent shaking or the Tsunami. From San Diego to Seattle, it was all destroyed by the tsunami.

The first earthquake caused the San Adreas fault to rupture big time from San Francisco to Los Angeles and that also caused much devastation, death and destruction.

And that triggered the New Madrid fault in southern Missouri to rupture big time and this earthquake destroyed everything from St. Louis to Memphis and beyond. This quake caused the Mississippi river valley to split wide open from the Gulf of Mexico to the Great Lakes, so much so that America was divided.

 And the people saw this as a judgment of God, BUT still they did not repent of their sins. Many blamed God and many even cursed God for allowing this to happen.

The east coast (I thought originally) was an asteroid.
BUT what I saw, what I was shown was like a mountain, like a rock on fire plunging very fast into the Atlantic Ocean.

Now you have the La Palma volcano, and already half of that mountain has already slipped over 6 feet down toward the ocean. Now the concern is that the volcanic mountain is unstable and could slide down into the Atlantic Ocean at any time.

The area of this slip is potentially the size of Manhattan and Trillions of tons of earth (on fire by the way from the active volcano) sliding into the ocean could cause catastrophic consequences for the East Coast of America.

A 100 ft. wave out in the ocean when it comes into the shallows it does what is called 'RUN UP' where the Tsunami wave grows taller in the shallow water, so the 100 ft. wave can now be 1000 ft.

If La Palma slips into the ocean, it will cause a wave at the island to be several hundred feet high at least.

Do you see the problem here?

Revelation 8:8 And the second angel sounded, and as it were a great mountain burning with fire was cast into the sea: and the third part of the sea became blood.

I am not always told what I am seeing, (I am just shown).

So, it is left up to me to interpret what I have been shown.
UNLESS the Holy Spirit gives me direction or interpretation of a dream.
I am left to my own understanding.

IT does NOT mean the dream is in error.
ONLY my 'interpretation' of WHAT I HAVE BEEN SHOWN is the error.

I am not a prophet I am only a lowly watchman with dreams and visions.

Not all things are revealed to me.
Sometimes God likes to keep things a mystery.
Give us little hints here and there.

But sometimes our understanding of what we have been shown is confusing to us.

1 Corinthians 13:9
FOR WE KNOW IN PART, AND WE PROPHESY IN PART.

1 Corinthians 13:12
FOR NOW WE SEE THROUGH A GLASS DARKLY.

Remember:

Isaiah 25:19 &20
The earth is utterly broken down, the earth is moved exceedingly.

The earth shall reel to and fro like a drunkard.

Isaiah 13:13
Therefore I will shake the heavens, and the earth shall remove out of her place, in the wrath of the Lord of hosts, and in the day of His fierce anger.

So, what can make the earth reel to and fro like a drunkard, remove the earth out of it's place?

A Tsunami with trillions and trillions of tons of water, (thousands of square miles of water) sloshing around in the Ocean, back and forth, like a rock being thrown into a pond, but on a much grander scale.

That is HOW you make the earth reel to and fro.

That is how you move the earth OUT OF IT'S PLACE.

All that weight from all that water sloshing around in the Ocean like a child in a bathtub sloshing water.

Now your next question is: Will this come to pass?

My dreams of the Time of Sorrows, the Rapture, the Tribulation have been given to me by the Holy Spirit.

And the Holy Spirit is never wrong.

The ONLY time I am wrong is when I interject what 'I THINK' Or what 'OTHERS THINK' and NOT what 'God thinks', that is what gets me in trouble every time.

This is why it is important to ONLY listen to God and not anyone else.

In my dreams I am always given confirmation as it was with this dream.

I was given these words: '**The sea is come up upon Babylon'.**

And that was all I was given, so from there I had to look up the entire verse to see what it said. And that was how I found Jeremiah 51:42.

Also, the Holy Spirit told me once (in an audible voice) that America was Babylon and America would be destroyed in one hour.

The Holy Spirit told me to read **Jeremiah 50, 51 and Revelation 18** (Maybe you should read it also.)

Deuteronomy 19: 15 At the mouth of two witnesses, or at the mouth of three witnesses shall the matter be established.

I had my confirmation and at the mouth of three witnesses.

The Bible, the Holy Spirit, my dream and you have David Wilkerson, Demetri Dudaman and many others .

Let me give you a scenario;

Let's say; 'I am living' on the east coast.

I look out my living room window and see the beautiful Atlantic Ocean before me.

All of a sudden, I see off in the distance a mountain of water rising up and heading to shore very fast.

(WHAT DO, I DO? JUMP AND RUN, SCREAM AND RUN FOR MY LIFE?)

NO, I DO WHAT THE PEOPLE DID ON THE TITANIC DID, I PRAY AND IN THE LAST SECONDS OF MY LIFE I PRAY POWERFUL, SINCERE, HUMBLE PRAYERS ON MY KNEES. I will pray like I have NEVER prayed before.

BUT I will NOT pray for God to save my life, RATHER I pray for God to save my soul.

So, what would you do?

Jump, run and scream with the crowd in terror?

And spend the last few seconds of your life screaming and running?

OR WOULD YOU BE ON YOUR KNEES PRAYING POWERFUL PRAYERS FOR GOD TO SAVE YOUR SOUL?

I believe at the last possible second Jesus will Rapture His faithful home and we will not even get wet.

Because we are ALL on the Titanic and this ship is sinking wither you realize it or NOT, this ship is sinking.

And we are all going down with the ship.

So where do you put your faith and trust?

Because IF you are in the Will and Grace of Jesus Christ, washed in the blood and born again you will not even get wet.

BUT PLEASE do NOT get caught as a luke-warm Christian.

Or a Christian in name ONLY following a false doctrine like Once Saved Always Saved or a church that only tickles your ears?

As much as God loves you, God has rules, laws and Commandments and God cannot break his own rules. Or He would not be God.

So, follow Jesus and NOT a faith or religion. (Where did God say judgment would begin?) IN THE CHURCH, because the church fell away from its first love and led the people astray and like dumb sheep they followed to the slaughter.

This is NOT every church but over 99% of them.

BUT, NOT ALL, as there is always a remnant who follow Jesus, they know what the scriptures say and they follow Jesus and His word.   And it is this remnant that will be saved when the wrath of God is poured out upon the land.

I say; DO NOT follow a faith, a religion, a man or woman and not even me.

BUT FOLLOW the only one who can save your soul from hell, who can save you from what is to come upon this dying world and that would be Jesus Christ and HIS word in the King James Bible ONLY.

The only way to survive what is to come – IS TO NOT BE HERE!

In other words, STAND on the Word, Stand in Faith in Jesus Christ and trust in God and His word that HE will save us from this dying world, just as He promised He would.

The Rapture will be a rescue mission.

Remember:

Matthew 24:22
AND EXCEPT THOSE DAYS SHOULD BE SHORTENED, THERE SHOULD NO FLESF BE SAVED; BUT FOR THE ELECT'S SAKE THOSE DAYS SHALL BE SHORTENED.

I am standing on the promises of GOD, what are you standing ON?

The same God who judged Israel HIS chosen people so very harsh is NOW judging America.

NOW is the time to humble yourself before Almighty God, repent of sin and beg the blood of Jesus wash over you and wash ALL your sin away, wash you clean and make you white as snow. And beg Jesus to enter your heart as your Lord and savior to lead you and guide you every step of the way.

As nothing else can save you, ONLY Jesus can save anyone.

YOU ARE STANDING ON THE TITANIC and this ship is sinking:
So what are you going to do?

NOW is the time to carry your Bible everywhere you can.

NOW is the time to say the Blessing over every meal you eat.

NOW is the time to repent of sin as sin is in everything.

NOW is the time to be in humble, sincere prayer.

God Bless you and God keep you and yours in His loving arms just like He held me.

May God open the windows of heaven and rain down blessings upon you until your storehouses are bursting with increase.

And we will see you on the streets of gold one day very soon!

WITH MUCH LOVE AND MORE GRACE FROM ABOVE

AMEN

CHAPTER TWENTY-ONE

My Titanic Dream

Now some would think a dream of the Titanic would NOT have anything to do with the Tribulation and I would agree with you. Except in this case there is a very important lesson to learn from this Titanic dream, so I will include it here.

I dreamed I was on the Titanic, and just like Leonardo DiCaprio, I too was standing at the railing at the back of the ship right when it was about to go down for the last time.

But in my dream, I was alone but there were other people lined up at the railing on either side of me (just like in the movie) and everyone was wide eyed and terrified.

When all of a sudden everyone started to pray and they prayed mighty, heartfelt and compelling prayers with all sincerity as NOW they had nothing but sincerity in their hearts.

As they knew their time was short for this world. They prayed and wept tears and prayed in earnest, compelling and powerful prayers.

I had never heard of such powerful and heartfelt prayers before and their prayers moved me and touched my heart.

But what impressed me the most was NOT ONE person was praying for God to spare their lives they were all praying for God to save their souls.

When times and conditions get at their worst and you see your end is before you, you need to remember to pray God save your soul and not your life.

Is your life that important?

BUT your soul, where IT spends eternity is the most important thing you could ever pray for.

So, if you find yourself in the Tribulation remember to pray God save your soul and not your life.

And DO NOT take the Mark of the Beast or worship name, his image or his number and NEVER deny Jesus Christ as your Lord and savior.

So much easier to give your heart to Jesus NOW and skip the tribulation and all of it's horrors of which there are many.

God Bless you and God keep you and yours safe in these last days.

CHAPTER TWENTY-TWO
Demon Possessed Run From Door To Door

I had this rather startling dream early on and as the years came more was revealed to me about this dream, things that were unexplained now made sense to me.

I was a fly on the wall so I guess I was there in spirit only and no one saw me or heard me.

But I saw and I heard everything.

What I saw was a family a man and a woman a father and a mother and they had a young boy and girl with them, their children.

It was in the winter time and it was so cold, it was bone chilling cold and everyone was shivering. The power had been off for a long time and there was no water, no power, no gas, and certainly NO HEAT. Now some people might have a little propane left or some might have some firewood left but those supplies were dwindling fast.

They had piled two mattresses on top of each other in the middle of the living room.

They got on top of the mattresses and then covered themselves with layer after layer of blankets over them while they were huddled together.

This way they could share body heat and keep it in under all the blankets, they allowed a small hole at the top so they could get fresh air.

And they were huddled together and they were still shivering almost violently.

Then my attention was drawn to the big picture window and I looked outside and what I saw gave me chills.

I saw a group of young men carrying clubs, chains, tire irons, knives and they were groaning and making guttural noises, not even talking but just making animal noises.

The way they ran and acted was not normal, they acted like those people you see on the drug called FLAKKA, and they could not comprehend, could not reason or think they acted on pure instinct.

They were very intent on doing what they were doing and that was to crash every door in, into every home and go inside and kill everyone at home and every animal too.

I saw them come to a door and they kicked it in with heavy boots and they ran inside very quickly. They killed everyone they found inside, they usually killed the men first and then you would hear a blood curdling scream and then SILENCE.

If they ran across a home that had any form of heat or food they might spend some time there or spend the night only to start their rampage again the next day.

I saw them, I heard them. They made animal noises and other noises that were impossible for any human to make. They contorted their bodies into shapes that were impossible for any human to get into.

They were perfectly possessed and their possession was complete. The demons in them took full control of them making them do unspeakable things.

They ate people alive or dead and ate animals alive or dead. I did not see them commit any sexual acts but I am sure they did such things on the living and the dead.

The cold didn't seem to bother them, being possessed they felt neither hot nor cold.

They were terrifying to see work without conscience, or any pity on anyone or anything.

These groups were small usually only 4 or 5 and maybe as many as 7 or 9 but they seemed to all have one goal and one purpose, to KILL with rigor.

Then my attention was drawn back to the family shivering under the blankets. And I saw them shivering so hard as it must have been painful to shiver so hard.

ONLY then did I realize they were NOT shivering from the cold; they were shivering from fear as their house was next.

This is also coming in the Tribulation, but I think it will be early in the Tribulation as many were still alive, and not all the homes were destroyed, not yet.

In the Tribulation people will go mad and riot, burn, kill, destroy everything goes crazy in this world of the future.

Family members will turn on family members and kill them for no reason, only that they are possessed.

In a world gone mad the fact that only a year or two before, there was plenty to eat, drink, wear, no one was cold or hungry, BUT now everyone was cold, hungry and everyone was a danger to you and to your family.

And as for children I have explained elsewhere HOW children even babies will end up in the Tribulation.

A horrific world is coming BUT you DO NOT HAVE TO SEE IT AND EXPERIENCE IT.

All you must do is repent of your sins and believe in Jesus Christ that He died for your sins on an old wooden cross, was buried and arose from the grave on the third day.

BELIEVE that Jesus is the Son of God who was sent by the Father to pay your sin debt and to offer you salvation.

Only His blood can wash away your sins.

God Bless you and God keep you and yours in His loving arms.

CHAPTER TWENTY-THREE

What The Holy Spirit Gave Me

About May 23, 2019 I had a dream where I went into the hospital for something very minor. But when I woke up I had several doctors bending over me telling me they were so sorry but they had to remove my left foot to save my life. I looked down at my feet and sure enough I saw only one foot under the covers.

I was shocked, how could this be, what happened. I was crushed. Now all I could think of was the fact I would have to spend the rest of my life in a wheel chair. My future seemed very bleak, to have to accept the fact that I would not be able to walk the rest of my life.

Then a few days later the Holy Spirit reminded me that a couple years earlier when I had refused to talk to my church congregation, that the Holy Spirit came to me then and told me that: "I did not need to walk to do God's will".

At that point I felt like something very important would be coming to me and that dream was another warning that I had better 'SPEAK' about this and tell everyone.

On the night of Thursday May 30, 2019 I had contact with the Holy Spirit and he told me something he wanted me to share with my church and with you.

I asked God to PLEASE give me a confirmation dream or something anything to confirm this message was from God.   But it had to be something significant a slap in your face and not something subjective or random. Something that could only come from God.

Well that very same night I got my slap in the face. I got two dreams back-to-back to confirm that what the Holy Spirit gave me was of and from God.

My first dream I was out doors in the country in the dark and the road was wet and a car came around the curve a little to fast and skidded off the road and crashed and then the car caught on fire. I saw this clearly in my dream.

Then that dream went dark and I became aware I was in a different dream. Where I was at my kitchen table and I had a knife in my hand and I was cutting a piece of tire from the car that had crashed and burned, to take into court before a jury and a judge.

I was going to be giving testimony and evidence in a court of law to show the tires were defective on the car that crashed and burned in my dream. And it was the defective tires that caused the accident and the subsequent fire.

I then realized that I was going before my church congregation to give testimony and evidence as proof of what the Holy Spirit had told me. My church congregation would be the jury and the Judge would be Almighty God as my witness of my testimony and my evidence.

That all struck me rather profound and that is when I realized that dream WAS my SLAP IN THE FACE I had asked for. My confirmation that would be profound and would be without a question from God.

I normally write out what I want to say and read it like a script. But this time that was NOT possible as my printer was broke and out of ink as well.

But still I wrote several pages and I read all of it and it sounded good but I knew that I could NOT remember all of it from memory to recite in my church.

I read over and over what I had written but then I decided that IF God had gave me this message that maybe God should give the message.

I prayed every single day that God put the words in my mouth that HE would have me speak. I would pray 'NOT MY WORDS BUT YOUR WORDS LORD". I also would pray 'NOT MY WILL, BUT THY WILL BE DONE'.

I got on my knees and I prayed and I prayed this prayer. I told the Lord that I would get out of his way and he could use me to give HIS message to the church.

To give me HIS words and to put HIS words in my mouth that I would speak. I prayed hard on this as I am NOT a public speaker, I stammer, I forget topics and words I need to use.

But NOT this time, it was like all I had to do was open my mouth and God started speaking through me. I spoke with power and authority.

I reminded the people that I was no one, I was just the dust of the earth and that no one was beneath me, BUT I was God's dirt and I would do as God commanded me to do.

I told of my dreams, my confirmation to speak and then I told them what the Holy Spirit gave me to speak to them about.

And that was, that NOW, RIGHT NOW we were in the Time of Sorrows, also referred to as Birth Pangs. And like Birth Pangs our calamities would intensify with frequency and ferocity just as in giving birth.

The evidence of my testimony was to read the Bible, be in prayer and watch the news as more and more calamities will come upon us!

And just like birth pains our calamities would come to us stronger and stronger and get more and more severe and would come to us closer and closer together right up to the Rapture of the faithful.

Then I said this:

Before one woe ends another woe begins!

As God comes to the wicked as an avenger, he comes to the righteous as a redeemer. Isaiah the prophet wrote 26:12 "The Lord is going to keep you in perfect peace – if you'll simply trust him".

The Lord says I haven't given you a spirit of fear but of power, love and sound mind. 2 Timothy 1:7.

Even in the most difficult of times we will enjoy great blessing because God will reveal himself as never before.

I finished with this: Remember God Is In Control

I don't always like talking gloom and doom but it seems the church is afraid to talk about what is coming. They don't want to offend young people who are planning on going to college and raise a family, buy a house and a car, get married and have so much of life to look forward to.

I sometimes think people look at me and think that I want to take that all away from young people.

The truth is I do not want to take anything away from anyone.
But I am here to tell you that if you are Raptured your life is only THEN just beginning.

You then have an eternity to look forward too without any of the problems of this world, like finding a job, marriage, divorce, sickness, death, operations, doctors, growing old, old age pains, having to work to provide for a family, not a tear, not a memory of pain or suffering. God will wipe away every tear and every strife from each and every heart.

As we will be going home. Home a place you belong, a place you came from but forgot. A place of peace, security, tranquility and much love. A place of indescribably beauty.
A place where the streets are paved with gold. And there is so much love and compassion there that it is indescribable love and joy.

I had a Rapture dream where Jesus came down to me and he put his arms around me. I wish there were words to describe how I felt being in the arms of Jesus.

But what I remember was that he never spoke a word to me but his eyes spoke volumes to me. What I saw in his eyes was pure love a love that transcends everything known about love, a love without bounds. But his eyes said something else, what his eyes also said were:

'I LOVE YOU AND I HAVE MISSED YOU SO VERY, VERY MUCH, WELCOME HOME'.

I wish I had never woken up from that dream and now I will spend the rest of my time on this earth trying to get back to the place where I was before HOME and back in the arms of Jesus. Where I belong and where you belong as well.

I think we all get to feel the arms of Jesus around us. I do not know how to explain it other than in heaven there is no time. So, there is time for everything, everything important that is.

My fervent pray is that we see you there on the streets of gold one day very soon.

One day the turmoil, strife and pain of this life will be swept away and we will be forever young in glorified bodies and we will live forever in paradise with our Father, His Son Jesus and the Holy Spirit, and all the angels and all the saints who went on before us.

God will wipe away every tear. No more pain or suffering.

No one ever grows old.

No one wears glasses or hearing aids in heaven

No one has any fake knees, hips or any other fake body parts.

And if you are blind or only have one eye you will have perfect vision and all of your missing body parts will be restored and function perfectly.

We will not need to walk, but we have feet.

We will not need to eat, but we will have food.

We will not need to breath, but we will have air.

We will not need to sleep or rest but we all will have mansions we call our home.

No one will ever get tired or have to sit down or take a break in heaven.

We will not have a sun as it is the holiness, the righteousness of God the Father who gives us our light and our warmth forever.

We will be in perfect glorified bodies as God is perfect, His creation in heaven will be perfect as well.

Only in that place will we finally learn to trust in God for EVERYTHING, EVERY NEED.

WITH MUCH LOVE & MORE GRACE FROM ABOVE

CHAPTER TWENTY-FOUR

God Speaks to me by Morse Code

I Think every Christian has had this happen to them, they get busy in their everyday lives and they put off praying, the next thing you know it's been days since you have prayed at all.

Then you notice that your prayers are not as heartfelt or sincere as they once were.

And you feel at a distance from God. THIS IS NOT GOD PULLING AWAY FROM YOU, THIS IS YOU PULLING AWAY FROM GOD.

About a year and a half ago, it's hard for me to recall how far back things have happened for some reason.

But I fell into this situation, and I felt terrible, that no matter how close to God I was, that I felt Him every day in my life and then all of a sudden, I felt nothing. I DID NOT LIKE THAT FEELING.

I knew what I had to do. I got on my knees at the foot of my bed and I cried for forgiveness. I begged God to forgive me for falling away from Him. I knew it was my fault and I begged for forgiveness.

I prayed for over an hour, then I sat on the side of my bed and with tears streaming down my face I cried and I begged for forgiveness, I felt so low, with all I have been shown, with all I have been given for me to fall away.

After a while of sitting on the side of my bed crying, for some time I decided to lay in bed.

When my head hit my pillow, I was silent, I was waiting on the Lord. It was no time and I started hearing an electronic tone through my pillow.

I remember when I was a kid, I would put my transistor radio under my pillow to listen to it without my parents knowing.

It was like that, it was loud, louder than just a ringing in my ear. It was an electronic tone coming from my pillow.
I wanted so bad to lift my pillow and see just what was under my pillow making that sound.

After only a few seconds I realized it was Morse Code I was hearing. BUT HOW WAS I HEARING MORSE CODE THROUGH MY PILLOW?

I didn't know Morse Code but I knew the concept behind it with dots and dashes. BUT this Morse Code was slowed down, in fact it was very slow and very deliberate.

It was a beep for a dot and a long beeeeep for a dash. (BUT what was it saying)!

I knew that between each letter was a short deliberate space of blank time and then the next letter would start.

I also knew that when a word finished there was a double space of time showing the end of a word.

But that was all I knew about Morse Code.

I followed the beeps and the dashes not knowing what the letters were or what the message meant.

There were a series of 4 letters and then a long pause that was followed by 3 more letters and then it stopped.

This was the message I got:

Beep, dash, beep, beep

Dash, dash, dash

Beep, beep, beep, dash

Beep

And here was a double long pause, and I waited to see if it would start up again and it did.

Dash, beep, dash, dash

Dash, dash, dash

Beep, beep, dash

Then it fell silent and it did not return.

I started praying, I reminded God that I did not know Morse Code.

Then in my inner ear and it was as clear as a bell the words:

LOVE YOU

I heard from God.

God knows my name, God sees what I do, and God knows the number of hairs on my head.

And God knows your name as well. God sees everything, God knows what you do and what you, don't do.

God knows your pain and suffering, your heart ache and God is with you, all you have to do is call out to Him and He will answer you.

In these Last Days God will reveal himself as never before.

Trust in God, believe in God, as He will never forsake you and never ever leave you.

You may step away from Jesus, but Jesus will never step away from you.

And NO, God may not answer you in Morse Code, but God is mysterious, surprising and He seems to never be the same twice when He answers you.

God is surprising, awe inspiring, Holy, Righteous and True and God's word will stand forever.

God is a respecter of no person.

And God will do all His pleasure.

The trick is to be pleasing to God, and to get God's attention.

To deny the flesh, is to release the spirit person inside of you.

These Last Days we all need to fast and to pray to be in the will and grace of Jesus Christ and to be pleasing to God above all things.

As no other name in heaven or on earth can save you, me or anyone from what is coming upon this earth except for the name of Jesus.

It's like a roaring in your ears, you can hear it coming but you can NOT see it yet. What you hear is a runaway freight train barreling down the mountain with no brakes. And it's headed straight at an immovable object (a wall) and when it gets there NOTHING and NO ONE will ever be the same again.

That immovable 'wall' is the Rapture and it's coming, we don't know when, we just know it's coming very soon. AS WE CAN HEAR THAT FREIGHT TRAIN AND IT'S COMING VERY SOON.

Have you noticed how it seems as if time itself has sped up?

You feel it every day getting closer and closer, you smell it in the air, you see it in the wind in the trees, you hear it everywhere around you, you see it on the news, you hear and see it in world events, EVERY WHERE, EVERYTHING IS REMINDING YOU THAT THE RAPTURE IS OH SO CLOSE.

No, God does NOT like being put in a box, and every time you try to put God in a box, He will get out every single time.

Remember that in these Last Days what you do and what you say is more important than you could ever imagine.

Please I beg you to carry your Bible everywhere you go and say the blessing over every meal you eat and repent of sin every time you pray.

Because in these Last Days is NOT the time to deny Jesus in any way, shape or form.

I carry my Bible everywhere I go, and I pray you do likewise.

We pray that Jesus takes you home at the Rapture because this world will be hell on earth after the Rapture and you do not want to be here for that.

There is NO surviving it, no matter how much preps you have, and no matter how deep your underground bunker your comfort will only be temporary.

HELL ON EARTH IS COMING – GET READY, GET PREPARED WITH JESUS THAT YOU MAY BE ACCOUNTED AS WORTHY TO ESCAPE THE TRIBULATION THAT IS TO COME UPON THIS VILE AND WICKED EARTH.

Because nothing else will save you.

I have been given much and I have been shown much, BUT I am nothing special.

I remain just a humble servant.

Who only seeks to please Almighty God.

I have no aspirations of wealth or fame; ALL I want is to Please my God.

And to that end I have done all that I have done.

God Bless you and God keep you and yours safe.
Yes bad times are coming, BUT we, who are in the will and grace of Jesus Christ, washed in the blood of Jesus Christ and born again HAVE NOTHING TO FEAR.

Something BIG is coming and it's coming very soon.

YES, Others may run to and fro and cry out to the rocks to hide them from the wrath of God. BUT I will not run and I will not hide, I will be on my knees praying that God save my soul.
As that is the most important thing.

Read your King James Bible as it is the ONLY true inspired word of God.

God Bless you and yours MIGHTILY

Chapter Twenty-Five

Evicted

I have had two dreams of being evicted.

My first dream I was home in bed taking a nap.

When all of a sudden, I was startled awake by a very loud and hard knocking and someone was yelling something at my front door, that I could not make out.

So, I jumped up and quickly got dressed, I went to the front door and I was shocked to see four police officers at my front door. I said Hello, can I help you officers.

Then I was given a court order paper demanding I vacate the premises immediately for arrears in my payment.

They told me I had only 5 minutes to pack ONE bag and they would escort me off the property.

I told them I had animals, and no way could I take them with me, they said to release them into the back yard with a dish of food and water on the back porch.

I was shocked, I thought how could I put my babies out in the cold with only a dish of food and water on the back porch. But that was exactly what I had to do.

I was told that once they escorted me off the property I would be arrested for trespassing IF I returned to the property.

They told me to hurry, and I ran and grabbed a pillow case and began to quickly go through my clothes and I was thinking I had no time for pictures, TV, stereo, silverware, dishes, NO TIME for anything but a single bag of clothes is all.

And all the while, I was quickly rummaging through my clothes thinking what I needed for the streets in cold weather and in hot weather as well.

While I was doing that the police at my door were counting down how many minutes I had, before they would come into my home and physically remove me from my home.

I was running around like a mad man trying to think and pack at the same time.

It was unreal, here I thought I would never be homeless, and here I was only now 2 minutes away from being homeless myself. Those people I saw on street corners panhandling for money, NOW I WAS ONE OF THEM.

I always thought that the government would step in at some point, when there were millions of homeless in America, I just always thought the president or congress would step in and stop the evections BUT they did NOT.

Now I was homeless but I was not alone.

In my second dream of being homeless, I was riding around in a car and I was being driven out of a city, and when we hit the city limit sign is where the homeless started to line the ditches, and this was every city, every town in

America. America had become a homeless nation, and it seemed everyone was homeless. There were the very old, men, women, children even babies.

The reason they were all just outside of town, was the fact that homelessness had turned into such a scourge all across America, that every city had passed ordinances making homelessness (vagrancy) illegal in every city and town.

So when you became homeless, you made your way to the city limits and camped out just outside the city limits.

This was not an isolated event, as it seemed everyone was homeless, all of America was homeless.

And if they caught you inside the city limits and homeless, they shipped you off to a FEMA camp, and after that no one ever heard from you again. You disappeared and you were never seen or heard from again.

I seemed to be seeing this in the spirit, and I saw this all across America that homelessness was everywhere, and it seemed everyone was homeless.

America was now living in the ditches just outside of town all across America.

This was a very sad sight to see.

The people looked beat and they knew it.

Many just gave up and went into town, and let the authorities take them away to the local FEMA camp, thinking anything was better than living outdoors in a ditch.

But it wasn't.

This is what I saw.

This is coming, but I am not sure if it is in the Tribulation or pre-Rapture, I just do not know.

But I thought that you should know.

God Bless you and yours MIGHTILY

Bad times are coming, and the only way to survive is to NOT be here.

As in being Raptured.

Safe in the arms of Jesus as there is no safer place to be in these last days.

CHAPTER TWENTY-SIX

Not The End – But The Beginning

Many people speculate as to who the antichrist is, and some people spend a lot of time and energy trying to figure out WHO HE IS.

I think our time and energy is more wisely spent in being Rapture ready, rather than to figure out WHO the antichrist is.

But when he comes on the scene, he will be very popular, charismatic, say all the right things, be very popular and a very handsome man. An accomplished politician and he will have many contacts and connections.

And he will speak with authority, and power as one who knows things and can get things done and many people will follow him.

He will seem to have all the answers to our problems, and everyone will love him.

He will seduce many with his tongue.

He will be seen as the savior to mankind and eventually will require everyone to worship him as God.

This will fully evolve at the 3 ½ year mark of his reign.

He will introduce a cure for all the ills of the vaxxcine and that will also make you live a very long time, be smarter, lean, free from almost every disease, faster, heal up from injuries super quick. This will be the Mark of the Beast.

And with that, he will be viewed as a god – the savior of mankind. And his popularity will grow and increase.

And he will demand to be worshiped as God and IF you do not submit to this you will be put to death.

The Bible says that Israel will stand alone in the Gog-Magog war. Remember **Jeremiah 50 & 51** and **Revelation 18** America will be destroyed, and this is coming and coming very soon. So, the Rapture must be very close now.

So, the antichrist will not rule over America as America will be destroyed. And that is why Israel will stand alone in its next great war. Only God will fight for Israel in the next war.

I have seen this; I was told this, and the Bible says this and also David Wilkerson, Dumitru Duduman, Henery Gruber and many others saw this and knew this as well.

Many other prophets and watchmen have seen this as well.

The Lord spoke to me. And said: that it was time for me to speak. You may not want to hear what I am telling you, but I will only tell you the truth, as God revealed it to me. I was NOT called to be popular or to be a millionaire, but to tell you the truth and that is what I will do.

I am not interested in money, fame, fortune, fancy cars, expensive homes or even big jet airplanes. I am ONLY interested in being pleasing to God. And THAT is my entire motivation.

I will not be bought or bribed with earthly things.

I lay up my treasure in heaven.

The future is truly frightening for those caught in the Tribulation. Believe me I do NOT want to be there and neither do you.

But I am afraid, that there will be many that will have to go through the Tribulation. And many people will get hurt and die.

I have no insight as to when the Rapture will occur, I ONLY know it comes before the Tribulation starts, so it must be soon.

It is the season, and the time is right, all the signs show it can and will come any time now, any moment.

I have been given so many hints such as: **We are but one breath away from the Rapture.**

And: **The last grain of sand from the hourglass of time has already fallen through the neck of the hourglass and is about to hit bottom.**

YES, WE ARE THAT CLOSE TO THE RAPTURE!

The timing of the Rapture is a secret, but God told us to watch for the signs, to recognize the season we are in. So, God wants us to know when we are getting close, very close, and to be prepared for his return.

Now is when Jesus asked us to be in constant prayer, and be looking up as our redemption draweth nigh.

I know a lot of people have been setting Rapture dates, so much so it has become a cottage industry, with many books sold, and many videos were made and lots of ads run and a lot of money changed hands.

So much so that a lot of Christians have been burned out, watching, hoping and praying for the Rapture. All I can say is **'watch the signs and watch Israel'.**

But PLEASE stay faithful to God, keep in prayer, be in the word of God, put on the full armor of God, and be watching for that blessed hope, that great catching away (of the faithful, as it is coming).

Now there is a convergence of ALL the signs, and Jesus said when you see all these things look up for your redemption draweth nigh.

Satan knows his time grows short, so he is busy causing as much havoc and destruction as he can in the little time he has left. And yes, that too is another sign. America is now so close to economic collapse, bank are failing almost daily now.

Yes, the signs are all there, so be watching, and in prayer for the Rapture (the Great Catching Away) of God's faithful to keep the Bride of Christ away from the hour of temptation and tribulation.

Revelation 3:10
Because thou hast kept the word of my patience, I also will keep thee from the hour of temptation, which shall come upon all the world, to try them that dwell upon the earth.

YES, the Lord wants you faithful and in prayer and watching for his return.

BUT ALSO, the Lord does NOT want you to quit working and planning for the future, (until you cannot). That day is almost upon us.

I know it's a double edge sword, and it's easy to fall into a nothing but 'watching' mode, BUT God does NOT want you to watch only and not work for the future.

SO yes, plan your kid's college education, go to school and work for your future as if you had all the time in the world. Plan future until you cannot.

BUT always remember also, to work in the Lord, as if it's your last day on earth to get lost souls to Jesus Christ. Do not put off talking to people about Jesus, especially when the Holy Spirit prompts you to talk to someone.

The Bible says: That the Lord will spew you out of his mouth if you are Luke Warm. You have to ask yourself, are you Luke warm? If so, It's time to pray and pray in earnest.

It's time for a Revival, it's time to talk to your family, friends, co-workers, knock on doors. How many doors have you knocked on lately?

Tell them that Jesus loves them, and Died for their sins. That their sins have already been paid for in blood, by Jesus.

I say it's sack cloth time my fellow Christians, it's time to get in your sack cloth and sit in ashes and pray like there is NO TOMORROW.

If this involves you putting on old rags and taking off make up, jewelry, fancy watches, rings (except wedding bands) anything pretentious or that says "look at me" and dumping your vacuum cleaner onto your bedroom floor and sitting it the dust and praying, you have to ask yourself "what is your soul worth and where will your soul spend eternity?"

I know over 300 prophecies were fulfilled in the Old Testament with the birth, life, death and resurrection of Jesus Christ.

I do NOT know how every single prophecy of our future in the Bible WILL be fulfilled.

I just know – IT WILL BE
We have God's word on it.

Psalm 91: 1-16
1 He that dwelleth in the secret place of the most High shall abide under the shadow of the Almighty.

2 I will say of the Lord, He is my refuge and my fortress: my God; in him will I trust.

3 Surely he shall deliver thee from the snare of the fowler, and from the noisome pestilence.

4 He shall cover thee with his feathers, and under his wings shalt thou trust: his truth shall be thy shield and buckler.

5 Thou shalt not be afraid for the terror by night; nor for the arrow that flieth by day;

6 Nor for the pestilence that walketh in darkness; nor for the destruction that wasteth at noonday.

7 A thousand shall fall at thy side, and ten thousand at thy right hand; but it shall not come nigh thee.

8 Only with thine eyes shalt thou behold and see the reward of the wicked.

9 Because thou hast made the Lord, which is my refuge, even the most High, thy habitation;

10 There shall no evil befall thee, neither shall any plague come nigh thy dwelling.

11 For he shall give his angels charge over thee, to keep thee in all thy ways.

12 They shall bear thee up in their hands, lest thou dash thy foot against a stone.

13 Thou shalt tread upon the lion and adder: the young lion and the dragon shalt thou trample under feet.

14 Because he hath set his love upon me, therefore will I deliver him: I will set him on high, because he hath known my name.

15 He shall call upon me, and I will answer him: I will be with him in trouble; I will deliver him, and honor him.

16 With long life will I satisfy him, and shew him my salvation.

Jesus is our ONLY salvation, he is the way, the life and the truth.

God Bless you and God keep you and yours in His loving arms

We will see you on the streets of gold on that day.

Watchman Tony Lamb

Revelation 20:4

And I saw thrones, and they sat upon them, and judgment was given unto them: and I saw the souls of them that were beheaded for the witness of Jesus, and for the word of God, and which had not worshipped the beast, neither his image, neither had received his mark upon their foreheads, or in their hands; and they lived and reigned with Christ a thousand years.

EPILOGUE

We are all blessed to be alive at this time in history to see the heavy hand of God deal with the earth. And to see and be a part of the Rapture, we are truly blessed. God chose us to be born for this time RIGHT NOW.

I have not included every dream as some were somewhat vague and to be honest, I have forgotten many more dreams than I have recalled here. I think the Holy Spirit has taken some of these dreams from my memory as to recall them all would be more than I could bear.

Though I have physical problems and ailments I am truly blessed as God chose me for this work. I was humbled by God to the ground and from the ground He lifted me up and set my feet upon His path.

And to that end I remain humble and true, just the dust of the earth and no one is beneath me, BUT I AM GOD'S DIRT!

As God comes to the wicked as an avenger, he comes to the righteous as a redeemer. Isaiah the prophet wrote 26:12 "The Lord is going to keep you in perfect peace – if you'll simply trust him".

The Lord says I haven't given you a spirit of fear but of power, love and sound mind. 2 Timothy 1:7.

Even in the most difficult of times we will enjoy great blessing because God will reveal himself as never before.

In the last days God will reveal Himself as never before.

This book is dedicated to:

Daniel,

Brian,

Crystal,

Zachary,

Paige,

Joshua,

Mason,

Mariah,

Sydney,

Rylee,

Tyler,

Tim,

Terry,

Julie,

Sarah,

Erin,

Tim Jr.,

John,

Diana

And many others unnamed. I love you and miss you terribly. I pray God keep you and make his face shine upon you and give you peace!

A NOTE TO MY FAMILY:

Please remember those who came before you who worked from sun up to sun down bent over all day long slaving away in hot Arkansas cotton fields until their fingers bleed, dragging 50 pound cotton sacks up and down the rows of cotton, JUST SO YOU AND I AND YOUR FAMILY COULD BE HERE TODAY!

Thank You

Mom and Dad (Marie Lamb and John Lamb)

See my new web site, I have tons of FREE stuff at: www.tonylamb.org

(I am not a Minister, Deacon or even a Sunday School Teacher)

But I am a born again, washed in the blood of Jesus,

A Watchman with dreams and visions for the soon return of Jesus Christ.

If you would like to contact me in regards to giving my testimony at your church or function (I do not charge a fee for speaking) email me at: watchmensreport(at)gmail.(com)

My physical address is: Tony Lamb, P.O. Box 41, Dardanelle, AR 72834

The new Azusa St. website is at: www.TonyLamb.org/AzusaSt.html

If you would like to see my many videos go to www.youtube.com and in the [search] box type in [Tony Lamb] and it should take you to my youtube channel page. Thank You

My other books include:

'GOD SHOWED ME THE FUTURE – America Is Entering Judgement'

by Tony Lamb

'MY DREAMS AND VISIONS – And Contact I Have Had With The Holy Spirit'

by Tony Lamb

'IN THE TWINKLING OF AN EYE' – I was Raptured and I received a new glorified body and Jesus held me in His arms and I looked into the eyes of God
by Tony Lamb

WHAT HAPPENS WHEN YOU TELL GOD 'NO' – I Am Just The Dust Of The Earth – But I Am God's Dirt'
By Tony Lamb

If you would like additional copies of this or any of my books go to my website or

go to: www.amazon.com

See our on-line store at: https://tony-lamb.myshopify.com/

See our website at: www.TonyLamb.org

Thank You

God Bless You

Tony Lamb

A humble Watchman and Servant

Of the Most High Living God

The God of Israel.

Who sits upon the Throne

Above All.

In Jesus name I pray.

AMEN